Copy Right

Understanding the art of Learning from others

JOBA ADEKANMI

Copy Right

Copyright © 2021 Joba Adekanmi

ISBN 978-1-914528-03-3

Published in United Kingdom by:
Impact Publishing House

All rights reserved. This book or any portion thereof may not be reproduced or used in any manner whatsoever without the express written permission of the publisher except for the use of brief excerpts in a book review, article, or magazine.

www.TheServantandKing.com
iph@TheServantandKing.com

Contents

	Preface	5
	Introduction	9
Chapter 1:	The Choice	15
Chapter 2:	The Possible Outcome	23
Chapter 3:	The Environment	33
Chapter 4:	The Goal	41
Chapter 5:	The Principles	51
Chapter 6:	Ask Questions	59
Chapter 7:	Connect	69
Chapter 8:	Consistency	77
Chapter 9:	The Fact	85
Chapter 10:	The Purpose	93
Chapter 11:	The Inverse	101
Chapter 12:	The Action	109
Chapter 13:	The Priorities	117
Chapter 14:	Cumulative Actions	127
Chapter 15:	The Multitudes	135

Contents

Chapter 16: The Responsibility	143
Chapter 17: Know or Do?	151
Chapter 18: I am Surprised	163
Chapter 19: The Scope	173
Chapter 20: The Use	185
Chapter 21: The Need	191
References	197

Preface

It is one of those experiences in life. Many have done it so well, some better than others. It has led to rewards, accomplishments, feats, victories, and probably a sense of fulfilment. However, it has become the undoing of many people because they lost their originality in the process. They have lost more than what they got, but many do not realise. What is it? You may ask. It is learning from others.

Humankind, regardless of race, colour, ethnicity, status, or nationality, has always learned from one source or the other. Everyone is a product of what they have chosen to learn.

How do we choose what we learn, and how does it affect our lives?

Many things influence what we do, how we do them and the circumstance under which we do them. Consciously or unconsciously, directly or indirectly, whether we admit it or not, I found it to be true.

Many years ago, a man visited his friend. As he walked through the yard, he observed something that caught his attention. He was fascinated; he thought for a while and uttered these words, 'It looks like a goat, but behaves like the dog.'

It was the case of a kid that grew up with a dog in a family yard. It was a struggle for him to come to terms with the reality before him. The kid, now a goat, seem to have lost some characteristics of a goat. The goat always followed the dog, reproducing every action and movement. It also began to eat poop like a dog, neglecting grass.

The dog was the source of learning for the goat, and the goat did all to be like it.

Interestingly, the dog could eat poop, although it may not be ideal, but there are many reasons for such behaviour. Its system could still process it to get some nourishment if the food was unabsorbed.[1] It would not cause harm to the dog, but the digestive system of the goat is different; it could mean danger.

The goat learnt from the dog, became a success in behaving like the dog, but it is not a dog; it has learnt to become something different.

I considered the story and wondered how many people have found themselves in a similar position in life. They have only learnt to be someone else and not themselves. Yes, they have succeeded in not being themselves. They later suffer the impact and consequences but never realise the problem.

This book is an attempt to reveal some important facts that many ignore, more often than not. They have learnt to be like others but lost themselves. We now have many copies but very few originals.

I hope this book will help you appreciate the numerous and diverse opportunities to learn—and how to maximise them in the context of your individuality and purpose. It will help you understand how to learn from others without losing your uniqueness.

Introduction

There are numerous challenges of humankind, but chief among them is the impact of what we learn without knowing and what we do without understanding the reason.

We live in a world with over 7.8 billion people living and many more that have died. It gives us a substantial opportunity to see examples of what we could become in people—living or dead. One or more of these people have influenced our lives one time or the other.

Yes, we copy what we see some other people do from the day we are born. It could be our parents, guidance, teachers, leaders, relatives, mentors, or friends. We could also copy those who are far away from us by reading, listening or watching them through the different media available.

Introduction

We consciously or unconsciously become like those we copy or those we learn from in some ways.

The influence of things we copy and people we learn from is quite powerful. It has a considerable impact, and it could make a significant difference in what we eventually become.

Have you ever paused to ask yourself, why do you do what you do? Why do you do it in a certain way?

You may have noticed a baby that feels excited about touching the contents of a soiled nappy while being changed. If the baby continues without any external intervention, it could end up in the mouth without any bad feeling. They probably think it is something worthy of taste or good for food.

However, the adults around would have a different feeling about the reaction of the baby. The baby, however, does not share that feeling at that time because the baby knows no better. As the baby grows older, the reaction is different. It is likely to be similar to those around at this time. It is because the baby learned from those around.

A child may be irritated by the idea of tasting or eating an earthworm picked up from a garden. It is because the child has been influenced by those around. It may have shaped how the child decides what to eat or not to eat. If everyone around reacts in a certain way and does not eat it, it might become acceptable to the child as good behaviour.

The baby, however, still in the process of learning, will not react in the same way as the baby will receive it with excitement and be happy to taste it.

What you do and how you do it could be a function of what you have learnt from someone else, consciously or unconsciously. We all copy because we have all learnt from someone, just like the baby, that enjoyed guidance from someone

Introduction

that helped develop a sense of hygiene and many other lessons.

As we grow, we have numerous opportunities to learn from different people, and we desire to copy, but sometimes we may not have achieved what we expected. Admittedly, we do accomplish it sometimes but could later discover it did not bring the joy or fulfilment we need.

How can we learn from others without losing our own identity or peculiarity? How can we learn from others and still be who we are? How can we copy and not lose focus of what we are to do?

How can we receive input from other people without destroying the reason for our existence? How do we decide what we learn from other people? How do we choose what we can or cannot copy? How do we ascertain that what we copy is right for us?

Like everything we do in life, we can also get it wrong. It has been the reason for so many unpleasant changes and experiences in the lives of many people.

The information we receive and how we accept them, whether it is right or wrong, eventually becomes what forms our beliefs, habits, routines, perception, views and lifestyle.

This book will help you consider some of your choices and probably help you make better ones. The world is wealthy, full of resources that has the potential to help you in life, but you should not use it against yourself. Come with me through the pages of this book, as I share some vital information—proven to be helpful—in learning from other people. I hope you will gain some understanding and apply it appropriately to your life and situation.

Introduction

The information we receive and how we accept them, whether it is right or wrong, eventually becomes what forms our beliefs, habits, routines, perception, views and lifestyle.

CHAPTER 1
The Choice

Learning is a lifelong adventure. The more we learn, the more we know. The more we know, the better the decisions we make. There is no limit or end to how much we can learn.

We all learn from different people at different times of our lives; there are numerous opportunities to do so. It could be those close to us like friends and family or many others that we can connect with in one way or the other. Yes, numerous opportunities to learn, but do we make the most of these opportunities?

There will always be someone to learn from because there will be someone that knows what you do not know or probably has a better understanding of what you have known.

Everybody has the privilege of people in life, and every one of those individuals has something to offer, which could translate to a positively or negatively change.

The world is full of people, all kinds of people which present us with a possibility to learn. We all have this global pool of human resources that could help in our life journey. There are so many sources available to get the necessary assistance to make the most of our lives.

Do you find any of the following statements familiar?

I wish;

I knew this truth 30 years ago.

I listened to my Father or Mother many years ago.

I employed that gentleman or lady.

I adhered to the guidelines of the fire officer.

I took the advice of security personnel.

I did not follow his counsel.
I never did what he did.
I never followed his footsteps.

Or I am glad;
I followed the instructions of my Father or Mother.
I left or kept my friend.
I followed his counsel.
I listened to my teacher.

Did you observe the different groups of statements? There is a wish that reflects a good or bad choice of the past. All these statements could be referring to several people at various stages of their life. All these people form part of the global human resources available to all. Everyone in life has varying experiences based on what they chose to learn and from whom they are willing to learn.

Many people look back to say some of these things. Sometimes it could be too late as they may be already experiencing the consequences of their decisions before perceiving the extent of the damage done. If you make the right choice, you can look back and be glad you did. If you make the wrong choice, you may have the opportunity to make amends and change your decision.

What guides the choice of who you can learn from or one that can help you? What influences your decisions?

We all have the power to choose—but when we use that ability—we also enjoy the result or consequences of our choices. Everyone desires to use this power to enhance their potential and not destroy or frustrate themselves. It will be helpful to know how to use it to your advantage and not to your hurt.

Everyone has something to offer regardless of their background or circumstances. Our prejudice may hinder us and affect our choice, which translates to not making the best choice. You could decide to disregard or despise the advice of a safety officer. It is a choice you could make, for instance, because he is not like you in some ways. It is based on prejudice and not what he has to offer; the result could be dangerous to you as your safety could at risk for ignoring the advice.

We can achieve more positive results if we understand the value of every individual and appreciate their contributions. There are many different characters, each with unique abilities—our preconceptions may not be a good judge of such resources—and they have a function and a role to play.

While everyone may not be correct all of the time, we still need to make choices on a case-by-case basis. Appreciating the global human resources as part of the help that can enhance our lives without being prejudicial can go a long way in making us better people.

You can learn from the poor as you can from the rich. Help can come from the famous as well as the unknown. It is possible to win battles with contributions

The Choice

from the weak or strong. Wisdom can come from the young as well as the old. Experts could make mistakes as well as the novice.

Those you less think of to be valuable could sometimes be the help you need. When we make the wrong choices, we are affected by it as our potentials could become limited.

The battle of Britain, which started in July 1940, was fought and won by the Royal Air Force pilots, using new generation fighter planes called Spitfire, which was crucial to the victory.

In 1934, Captain Fred Hill, a scientific officer in the air ministry, persuaded that each new generation Spitfire and Hurricane fighter planes needed more than the four machine guns in the initial design; he sought assistance on the issue. He decided to consult his thirteen-year-old daughter, Hazel, a talented mathematician. The pair were able to prove that eight machine guns on each plane was essential for success. They worked together using mathematical calculations, each one contributing to achieve the goal. He was able to convince his superiors to use this discovery in designing the RAF's aircraft.[1]

The government changed its mind because of Hazel's calculations. Victory for the nation came from the bravery of the pilots. The contributions of so many other people, including this young teenager, made a difference. The little input affected the outcome. Even though the girl was not a pilot, she played a role in the success.

Her father was able to see the value and made a choice to learn from her regardless of age and other factors that could have hindered him from benefiting from what she had to offer. Imagine if the father did not consult her daughter or if the government did not consider the input. It may have been a national disaster. The resource was available, but it would have been a matter of the wrong choice based on prejudice.

The Choice

What you need is available, but it could be in someone that does not look valuable to you. You may have been looking away or ignoring some resources that could be of help to you. Everyone has something to offer regardless of what they do, where they live, their financial situation, and so on.

If you want people to accept the principles by which you live, remember that your choices have corresponding results or consequences that may affect you and others. You do not have to suffer alone in frustration and depression. There is someone out there that can contribute to your victory or freedom.

You have the privilege to take advantage of the various opportunities to benefit from others to make the most of your life. You have the power to choose; you have many to choose from, so choose right so you can maximize your potential. The choice is quintessentially yours.

CHAPTER 2

The Possible Outcome

Life is full of choices, and we make a lot of them every day. However, every choice we make in life has implications that could be positive or negative. The outcome of what we do is very crucial and worth careful consideration. It could go a long way in helping us make better and informed decisions.

You should not only focus on what you are doing now or what you are copying but also the outcome of the actions you have chosen to follow. If you are happy to copy or follow a particular course in life, are you aware of the consequences of that choice, if any? Do you know what the likely result would be? Do you have an idea of the endpoint of such actions? If you are, Is that

The Possible Outcome

where you would like to be? Will you be happy with such an outcome?

It is not uncommon to find people copy someone without looking into the result of such actions. They may have some feelings, attachment or persuasion that has energised them to follow suit with limited or unclear facts about the implications. It may look neutral, pleasant, exciting, harmless, or innocent, but the results sometimes become a surprise. What can you do to avoid unpleasant consequences and such surprising experiences?

There are uncertainties in life and many situations that we cannot control. It may not be possible to ascertain the outcome of every situation. Notwithstanding, there are so many situations that repeat themselves such that the same actions usually have the same result in most cases.

You can observe the outcome of others. If everyone that performs the actions, most often than not, end up with the same or similar way. If you, therefore, follow the same steps, you are likely to end up with the same result. Knowing this could help you decide to accept or refuse to copy or follow that line of action or idea.

Early on Christmas morning, some years ago, I dropped off a neighbour of ours at the train station. On my way back, I saw a Mercedes Benz car, lying upside down on a dual carriage road, with enough evidence around, including many road signs destroyed because of an accident.

I parked safely, like some other road users, to see what I can do to help. As I walked towards the car, I saw the young lady partly covered in blood. While awaiting the arrival of the ambulance, someone suggested that her parents be informed. Sober, in pain and with a deep sense of guilt, she asked for a mobile phone as her phone lacked battery power.

She was reluctant to call her parents as she was scared. On the phone to her parents, they could not believe what has happened to their daughter and car on a

The Possible Outcome

Christmas morning. Their daughter kept saying, 'Sorry Mum, I was drunk, I was drunk.'

She must have learnt the act somewhere or from someone, but she did not realise that one of the possible outcomes just happened to her. Many people enjoy the present time and never see the consequences of their actions in the future. The same actions usually produce the same or similar results. So many lives have been lost or shattered in this way. Some have incurred losses and damages that are irrecoverable. It is possible to avoid such unpleasant moments by being careful when learning from other people.

Worrisome statistics abound globally of fatally injured drivers linked to alcohol; twenty per cent in high-income countries, to seventy per cent in low-income countries. The choice to engage in the action is a choice to agree to the possible outcome. The same activity usually produces the same result.

It is a dangerous thing to be engaged in anything without knowing and understanding the possible outcomes. Whatever the action is, everyone that has done the same in the past would have had some result. It becomes a possibility for everyone that engages in the same thing.

You may find out that many that spend time reading and preparing judiciously for their tests or examinations with relevant materials do well. The same actions will usually produce the same or similar results.

Many young people copy various activities because someone somewhere is doing it but never know that it is an action that has a possible outcome, just like every action. It is not a good idea to do what other people do; you do not know where there are going.

I once spoke to a young lady seeking admission into the University. She told me her desired course and location; I then asked her the reason for her choice. I was perplexed by her answer. She said, 'I chose

The Possible Outcome

the University and the course because my friend is doing the same in that location. I want to be where she is.'

It is like saying anywhere, any course, it does not matter. The destination of your friend may not be your destination. You may enjoy friendship now; that does now mean you will always find fulfilment where she is going. Everyone is unique, and you must identify your path and work towards getting to your destination.

Your desire could be to become a Doctor, Lawyer, Engineer, Scientist, or any other thing that will bring you fulfilment. There is a route or a path that leads there. Many have followed the right track and arrived at their destination. If you do not follow the right direction, you are likely to find yourself somewhere else.

Consider yourself going to the airport to board a plane to Heathrow in London from New York City. You must check that you are boarding the correct aircraft going to your destination, not just any available aircraft. If you do not, you are likely to arrive at a different destination. You may be landing in Australia instead of London. If you follow without understanding the outcome, you are likely to have some unpleasant surprises.

Every action follows a course that leads somewhere. Many people do not want the destination they eventually find themselves but unfortunately, just like a bus, train or aeroplane, you get on board by your choice and then transported to the destination advertised. If you do not check and confirm the details, it will still take you there. You have exercised your choice by getting on board, but in the end, you will not be happy to find yourself where you do not want to be.

There are so many examples around us of actions and their possible outcomes. You can make informed choices by checking the result of the action before you follow it. Whatever you decide to follow, make sure

The Possible Outcome

you understand the course you are on and the destination.

Ask yourself these sincere questions, where will this action take me? Where will I end up? Where do people that do such things end up in life? If the destination is not attractive to you, then change the course, and change the action. It will change the destination as well.

Do not copy others because what they are doing looks cool. It could be a temporary enjoyment that could lead to many lasting regrets if you do not make changes on time. Pause and think of where you desire to be in the future. Take some time to find out how to get there and put in the required actions. It will help set your feet on the right path and increase your chances of arriving at your destination.

Every action will lead you somewhere, but it is up to you to check and confirm if that is where you would like to be. Do not follow except you know where the path leads. Do not just copy anyone you see; you are unique, and you could be the best of you. There is a future for you, and you must get there.

It is a dangerous thing to be engaged in anything without knowing and understanding the possible outcomes.

CHAPTER 3

The Environment

Have you ever wondered why some people fail in seemingly profitable businesses? Why do many lose when everybody seems to proclaim profits? Why is it that what usually works does not work for some?

The same actions but different results. The same input but varying output. Have you ever witnessed such? Has it ever occurred to you why so many people try to do what others do and never get the same result? Have you wondered why some get frustrated because they expected one result but got the exact opposite? They desired profit; they got losses instead. They hoped to attract more people; they ended up with less. They thought it would turn out all right, but it did not. Why do we experience such conflicts and variations even when it seems the action looks the same?

You may have had the privilege of seeing two different people doing the same thing but end up with two different results. It probably might have happened to you at some point in your life, where you got a different outcome even though you did the same thing you had once done before. The difference could be a minor variation from the previous or probably, the exact opposite. You may have found this to be true. There is something different that may seem insignificant, but it is usually a strong determinant.

Let us imagine you are walking about fifty meters behind a friend on the street, and he then drops a twenty-pound note on the floor. During daylight, it would be easier for you to spot it as you walk towards the location. If it occurred at night time with no artificial source of light, the experience would be different. The money would still be on the ground, but you may not notice it. Some factors made it visible during the day, so there was success, but they were absent at night, so there is failure.

Similarly, ice cubes from a freezer thrown outside the garden in London will melt quickly in the summer compared to wintertime, even though it was from the same source and in the same place. The temperature and other factors of the same environment has affected the ice and has made it respond differently at different times. These, amongst others, are factors in the background that has altered the result.

You may have witnessed the actions of a farmer as he drops a seed in the ground. Simple and easy to understand? I wonder what you think. An attempt to copy without further details of the environment may end up in a different outcome. A change in the soil or ground will alter the output or process of germination or growth. The season could make a huge difference. The nutrients present or absent in the soil will

The Environment

reflect on the outcome. All of these factors and many others would have played a role in the success of the farmer. Anyone trying to copy him must also be aware of these factors and not just some actions. That is what I consider as the environment or factors that affect the outcome.

You may observe a farmer when they do their work. It is crucial to look at not just the activity but also the contributing factors. You may have a different result when there is a change in the circumstance or environment.

We often desire to copy the activities of some people hoping to get the same result they achieved. We, however, fail to realise some background information that helped them. Why, when and under which circumstance they performed such actions.

I have seen so many people lose their hard-earned money in a bid to copy what some investors are doing or advertising. They take the actions but do not consider the context, and they end up with a different and painful result. Investments will not always bring profits even if you bought them as low as they could be. There are so many other factors that come to play in achieving success that you need to understand to get the desired result. Those are the environmental factors that make it go well.

Love and discipline of children have produced different results in different circumstances because it is not just the actions that count, but also the understanding of the varying situations and knowing which is applicable and when. It is vital for success. Some children did not get disciplined when it was required and have become unruly and ungrateful. Some others have been starved of love when it was necessary; they turned out to be wild. Many often copy others; they only seem to be told or see when one of these is done and may not be privy to the activities at other times. There are so many factors that

The Environment

contribute to the success that is in the environment.

The success or failure of anyone has more to it than just some actions. Many other things around them would have played one role or the other in what they now see.

I once listened to a property investor that proclaims he always makes a profit from property. I soon found out a few things about his environment and what contributed to his success. He only buys repossessed properties—usually at a discount of thirty per cent or more of the market value. It implies that he is already in profit from day one, even if the market value does not change. Some people copy and invest in property; they buy at market value, a little more or less, which they may also see as a bargain; but they soon end up with a different result.

Students that pass or fail an examination most often than not have access to the same materials, but there are still differences in the result, most of the time. There is something more that has contributed to the success or failure of the students. Some of them could be traceable to factors around their environment.

Some new products have a significant interest in a short time after launch. The manufacturer of the product may already have a customer base. It could have been grown for a while or diverted from another business or service they were once involved. They could provide offers, discounts, or gifts and incentives to encourage and generate such interests. There are so many that invest in marketing through their contacts to spread awareness. Some people never consider these and keep struggling to make headway. There is more that goes into it than is usually seen.

Many are the things we can learn, but it is vital to understand the circumstances around the actions and the context. Their result is not just because of what they did. How, when, and the environment or

The Environment

prevailing conditions at the time they did it also matters. They all have a contribution to the result. Do not copy blindly. Some details in the surrounding circumstances are crucial to the success of the action, it may not be obvious, but that is what will make it work.

CHAPTER 4

The Goal

I once alighted from a train at Fenchurch Street station many years ago. As I walked through the ticket office, I found a young man handing out 'free' yoghurt pots to everyone. The first thought was why. What is he or the company he represents trying to achieve? What is their goal? I soon found out their intent.

One of the lessons you will learn in executing any project is to have a goal or objective and then work towards achieving it. It is not the other way round. You may have seen actions that are similar many times but aimed at achieving different goals. Also, they could be activities that are different but geared towards the same objective.

The easiest way I found to explain this is to try to answer the question, 'What do I want to achieve by doing this activity?' For every action you copy or desire to copy, you should be able to answer that question in sincerity to yourself. If you decide to follow a successful lawyer and become one, you may not understand his goal and therefore not understand what he sees as success.

Assume his goal is to help the helpless get justice, and he eventually became famous and wealthy as a result. Many others may copy him and become prominent and affluent, but their goal is to have wealth, not to help. They have a different aim even though they may both have wealth.

Moreover, it will be evident in the process because the actions will be towards the goal. One wants to help, but the other wants wealth. The lawyer becomes fulfilled when the helpless gets justice. He succeeds or achieves when that happens, but on the other hand, those that copy him will not be happy just because they get justice. It is the fame and wealth that matters the most to them. They will never count justice as success until they become rich and famous because it was never their aim.

There are so many times we see people invest in charities because of their desire to help people. They may get acknowledged, rewarded or famous as a result. Conversely, some copy them with a different goal in mind, which could be to become famous, get tax relief, get rewarded, take advantage of vulnerable people or get a position of CEO with fat salaries. The goal determines the actions that follow—the activities do not necessarily tell us the aim. One gets satisfaction when the needy get the help they need, while another is not happy until they become known, affluent, acknowledged or rewarded.

You may have seen so many people and love to do what they do, but you may struggle to understand why they do what they do or what they intend to achieve. A student may volunteer his/her skills or time to help and learn his/her desired skills within an organisation. The aim is to get juicy opportunities within the organisation or connections that could help with progress. On the other hand, an employee may also do the same thing. The goal could be to contribute or give back to society or help others that are in a vulnerable position. It is the same thing, but the aim differs. One achieves or becomes fulfiled when there is pay, job or appointment, but the other, at the opportunity to contribute and help the vulnerable.

What you desire to achieve determines what you do and how you do it. You work from the goal because you have to start from it and then decide on the action required to achieve it. If you engage in just any activity without a goal in mind, you may get results, but it may be meaningless, worthless or even destructive to you.

Many students have good grades in school, but it does not mean anything to them because there was no goal. Some work hard to acquire degrees and certifications, but they are confused even after having the highest qualifications because there was no goal. They get the certificate, then wonder, 'so what can I do with it or what do I do next?'. The only aim they probably had was to get the certificates because everybody seems to be doing the same.

If you do not have an end in mind, you may never know fulfilment—you would not know when you get there. A lot of people copy others and achieve something. They remain unfulfilled because they never had a goal. There was no end to look forward to, neither was there any way to have a sense of satisfaction. They do not even know when or by what to measure what they have achieved.

Goals are helpful but could also be destructive. It could also mean achieving one thing at the expense of so many others. A lady may attempt to do a job usually done by a man to prove that a lady can do it. If she succeeds, it could mean some other things have suffered for her to achieve her goal. The same could also be the case for a young man. A teenager could disobey the law to prove to his friends that he is daring and fearless. Many people indulge in reckless behaviours to please a few, make others happy or feel accepted. There are so many young lives behind bars because of this type of goals. They copied, but their aims were wrong, and they ended up in trouble. What do you want to achieve? Why do you do what you do?

What you copy should be a function of what you want to achieve. Check the goal before you copy from others. The action may look good or impressive, and the result may seem pleasant, but the goal or objective for doing it may be different from yours. The aim may give a different meaning to the actions.

Have you ever wondered why some people do what they do? Why do you get 'free' yoghurt pots from a train station? Why do you get free vouchers from your favourite store? You may have witnessed people with the same or similar actions but with a different goal. There is usually an aim behind what people do. I found that the 'free' yoghurt pot was not 'free' but a way of marketing the new product to create awareness and generate interest.

A traveller in medieval times came across three stonemasons in the course of his journey. He approached the three of them one at a time with the same question. The question was simple, 'What are you doing?' Their answers reveal what they intended to achieve by doing what they were doing. It exposed their goal. The first man answered, 'I am cutting and laying down stone, I can't wait to finish.' The second stonemason responded, 'I am building a wall. I am grateful to have this work so I can support my family.' The third had the opportunity to answer the same question, and he said, 'I am building a cathedral.' They were all doing the same thing at the same time.

The first wanted to have a job and get paid for what he does. That is the end of his goal. He is happy and satisfied when that happens.

The second was different—he desired a career and a means of livelihood—to support his family and probably meet all his expenses. That is why he does what he does daily. He is excited and fulfilled when he achieves that goal.

The third also differs from the others—he wanted to be part of history and a lasting legacy by contributing his quota for the benefit of future generations. His goal defines the reason behind what he does. He would not be worried about the pay or the career. The contributions he can make that will live after him gives him a greater sense of satisfaction.

It is the same activity—using the same type of skill—but different goals. They also have the same initial reward, but the satisfaction of each one differs.

John F Kennedy once visited NASA, and he saw a young janitor mopping up the floor. He asked him, 'What is your job?' He replied, 'I am helping send a man to the moon.' His goal was more than a job or career. He was contributing his part in his little way towards the future.

We all do so many things, and we can learn from so many things other people do, but it is very vital to have a goal and work towards achieving that goal. If you set a goal, focus on it, there will be a different approach to what you do, even though it is the same as some others. You can also find out why people do what they do. It will help you make better choices on what you copy and how you copy from them.

You may not always know what other people would like to achieve by what they do, but you should know your aim. You can set your own highest goals based on your future and desired destination. Be wise and first check to see if you have similar objectives. The energy that fuels the actions of people is a function of their goals. Let it come first, and then the activities that follow will be powered and sustained by it.

Declare objectives that will lead you to your great future, not one that will rob you of it. Do not copy others without understanding—set your goal and work towards it—they might have a different aim which could lead to the wrong destination.

CHAPTER 5

The Principles

Everyone desires to be like the great and successful people. Do we know what they have done or the price they have paid? Do we know what guides their actions or what fuels the way they operate? What is it that they do that is usually not visible to all? What is it that goes on in secret—that is responsible for the success we see in the open?

You may have wondered why some people succeed in one thing and others that try to do the same fail. A Businessman may be doing well, but those that want to do the same business fails. One athlete outperforms so many others. A pianist plays with so much mastery that an auditorium filled with thousands of people wonder in admiration.

Many times we see millions of people watch the award ceremony of sportsmen and women in various competitions. There is sometimes a desire to be in the same position and being the one to receive the award. I have seen many try with determination to be like some of these, but they never seem to succeed. Some people wake up with a resolution to register for such competitions as they feel, 'if that man can, I sure will be able to do better.' They soon realise there is more to it than a desire.

I have seen many lose their life-saving in an attempt to invest because someone else has had some returns on their investment. They anticipated the same or a better result, but they found themselves in a worse position, losing everything they have. What could be lacking? What is missing?

Principles, among other things, are vital in life. They are fundamental truths or laws which remain the same. People may change, but they do not change. If you follow the underlying principles behind a successful person, you will get the same result even if the man decides otherwise—they will still deliver the same outcome.

There is usually a principle that guides what people do and the results they get. They will generally lead to the same outcome if it is well understood and applied.

Gravity is an invisible force that makes any particle of matter fall freely. It remains constant. When you throw a stone up in the air, it will come down. Whenever you jump up, you will come down. You can easily repeat the result if you understand the principles.

It is common to find that people ignore principles—they focus on every other thing. They get frustrated when they do not get the expected result. They are crucial because they are constant and can help you reproduce the same outcome.

The Principles

The secret of every man is in their stories, and with a careful look, you might be able to get the principles responsible for their output.

Sportsmen and women spend hours daily in practice and rigorous exercise—in preparation for competitions that are years ahead. If you want to be one, you have to put in the hours, enjoy the discipline, appreciate the sacrifice and wait for your labour to produce fruits.

Many people that achieved their goal have had similar principles of hard work, integrity, sacrifice, self-denial, tenacity, courage, focus, and many others that have helped in their journey.

You are likely to do well in your examination if you study judiciously and understand the relevant materials. If you invest the hours and gain mastery of the subject matter, you will do well. No one is better than another. Everyone is a function of how well they have followed the principles they believed.

A big organisation once recruited two employees to a Marketing officer role. They both started work at the same time, level and remuneration. One decided to do extra by putting in the hours for development outside his hours of work. He spent extra time—learning and applying the principles he learnt from some others that have gone ahead of him in the industry. Eventually, his work became outstanding, and he earned himself a promotion for his efforts and the impact the positive changes have had on the organisation.

On the other hand, the other colleague was furious when the news was made public. He decided to make a formal complaint to the management for the 'unfair' treatment. They decided to invite him for a similar interview and asked the same questions. He got an invitation soon afterwards to compare the answers in the presence of the interview panel. He then realised that even though they started the work on the same day, his colleague has done so much more and added so much value that made him a better candidate for the promotion. If you add value to yourself, you will be worth much more; it is a principle that is always true.

Many organisations that succeed invest so much in customer service. They value their customers—they are truthful and sincere to them. They provide help and support for the products they sell. They make the customers happy as much as they can. That is one principle that helps to keep customers—it works. If you buy a product from a company that is willing to take it back if it fails, you will glad to buy from them and probably tell others. If they do not, you are likely to go somewhere else because their product has failed and they have refused to take responsibility for it. You may have found this to be true.

Many people you see around and envy have some principles that have helped them in life. You may never get the result they achieved until you learn and understand the principles behind their actions and apply them correctly.

Principles are vital but are not always easy to follow. It takes determination to scale through the threshold of resistance. You must be willing to give it all it may take to get you to your expectation or destination.

Great men stick to their principles and value them more than money. You will find out that many that have stood the test of time have great truths in common. You can learn better from others when you understand the underlying principles that have helped them and not just copying the actions you see.

There is usually a principle that guides what people do and the results they get. They will generally lead to the same outcome if it is well understood and applied.

CHAPTER 6
Ask Questions

One of the ways to get accurate information is by asking questions. Everyone would have asked one or more at different times in life. We might indeed have asked several questions, but there may be times we do not ask or probably not the right questions in life.

Have you ever asked the reason behind the actions of some people you so much love and respect? Have you assumed or probably surprised by their actions when it is different?

It is common to see different people act differently under the same circumstance. You may never know why someone behaves the way they do or their choices until you ask them. Your discovery could either confirm your thought or shock you.

There is a growing desire to do what others do, especially those seen as the great, accepted and successful. We may discover some shocking truths if we know the reason behind what some of these people do. The explanation could be different from what we think. Some people may think they know the reason for everything that happens—it is not always true. It is necessary to ask the right questions to get a better understanding of not just the actions but also the reasons behind them.

Little or no knowledge about something could be clear evidence of assumption. If we do not seek the correct and comprehensive information, we could misjudge and make wrong decisions. We often operate in error because of incomplete information and therefore end up with a different result.

There was a young professional that travelled very often to different destinations at different times as he wishes. A friend asked, 'Why do you travel so often, and where do you get the funds for these expensive trips.' He answered by explaining the nature of his work. 'I travel very often because of my work. The organisation I work for pays for the flights and accommodation by reimbursing all my expenses. I registered for a loyalty programme with the providers of the flight and accommodation. It means that I get loyalty points every time I use their services which then adds up to points that could give me a free ticket to different destinations and accommodation.' He was not paying for it with his own money. It was only a by-product or benefit he is enjoying because of the type of job he does. His friend had a change of mind because he knew better after the answer.

The young man may look prosperous to many people, spending so much on travels

Ask Questions

around the world. Some may think he is wasteful or dubious. The answer to the question will be of help to so many in doubt. He is taking advantage of the season of his life. He would not always be working for the same organisation or have the opportunity or privilege forever. The benefit was available to him and probably some others in a similar industry with similar organisational policies. A desire to be like him without understanding may cost much more. The young man was able to do all he did at little or no extra cost to him.

Many people copy this type of actions. They never realised that the people they are copying are driving company cars, living in company accommodation, clothed with allowances from their organisation, dining with vouchers or fully paid or claimable expenses, spending from trip allowances provided by their company or organisation. If you do not understand, do not assume. You will learn more from asking than copying without asking the right questions.

A lady once relocated because of her work and decided to sell her old house to buy a new one closer to her workplace. She found the right one, which was bigger, better and cheaper than the current one. There were many offers for the property as it generated many local interests.

The lady decided to offer more money compared to the others so that she could secure the property. It meant it was sold slightly higher than the asking price and the valued price. Asked, 'Why are you willing to pay more?' She said, 'It is still cheaper for me compared to my former property that I sold. I received some compensation from my company for the relocation. I also desperately need a place very close to work as soon as possible.'

The homeowner next door might attempt the same process—thinking that it will also sell above market value. It may not be so because the scenario may not be the same at that time. If only we can get to know more before we act like other people do, it

Ask Questions

will go a long way in helping us avoid some unpleasant experiences.

You may never get to know why people do what they do till you ask. If you want to learn, ask—then you can make informed decisions based on the answers.

Someone may relocate for many reasons. It could be a new job, to upsize or downsize, proximity to friends and family, moving away from troublesome neighbours or environment, compensation or a discount, accessibility to Schools, new opportunities and so on. If you move because everyone you know is relocating, you may later discover that you have done yourself a big disservice. The action could look good, but their reason for doing it may not be relevant to you. It could later lead to frustration if you follow the same step uninformed.

Some may go on expensive holidays because they have fewer financial commitments or have more support from their grown-up children. Some may decide to go on less costly holidays because they have more financial obligations at that phase of their lives. Some could opt to go on expensive trips even though they have more commitment but see it as an investment in education necessary at that time while depriving themselves of something else. Everyone may have a different reason for doing the same thing, but you may never know until you ask.

An employee was always early to get to work. When asked for the reason, he had a helpful answer. He revealed that he got a free ride to work from a neighbour that picked him up from home at a particular time which saves him a lot of money on transportation. He took advantage of the ride every day. It means that he arrived early every day. One may assume he is dedicated because he walks in an hour before work, but upon inquiry, the reason was different, which may soon be apparent when the free ride stops.

Another employee would not go home on time and kick against any offer to work from home. Asked for his reason; He revealed that there were some problems at home he was trying to avoid by staying longer at work. One could have assumed that he is hard-working, but not really.

A student could be quiet in a classroom because of the fear of shame if he makes a mistake. The teacher may assume he is gentle or well behaved and admonish other students to be like him. If asked, so many issues affecting him could come to light. He may not be gentle but probably going through so much that he could not voice out.

A popular speaker once walked to the stage to deliver a speech. She noticed that all eyes were on her shoes. It is probably well known and expensive. She decided to comment and said, 'I did not buy it—it was a gift.' Some people ruin their lives or put themselves under unnecessary pressures trying to wear what others are wearing, but they never know how they got it. It may be expensive, but it may be a gift, borrowed, hired, on loan, bought from savings, dividends, salary after hard work or extra work and so on. Be happy with yourself and the phase of life you are in at the moment. You may not be where they are yet—you may be there in a few years. Be patient.

You may be attracted to people by what you see. There may be a desire to do what they do. You may be missing something vital until you ask. You may not know the missing link until you inquire. You will be able to make a better decision when you are informed. You will understand more when you ask. Do not live based on assumptions; it could be very costly. Get relevant information that can help you see a transformation.

You can learn better from others when you understand the reason behind what they do by asking relevant questions. They will reveal the reasons behind their choices. It is worth waiting for because it will help

Ask Questions

you understand the reasons behind the actions. Ask before you copy.

CHAPTER 7
Connect

One of the truths you may have found in life is that, at every phase, there are three major categories of people. The first group have more knowledge or experience than you in a particular field or activity. The second are those that are at the same level, and the third group are those that have less knowledge or experience. It could apply to any profession, business, sport, skill, or activity.

You may desire to be better at what you do and probably find someone that does it better. That is a good start. You are then likely to discover a gap between where you are and where you desire to be. That gap could be as a result of so many things. The other person must have done or have them, but you have neither done nor have them.

It is possible to fill any of such gaps, but many attempt to do so by trying to start from where they are not or neglecting where they are at the moment. Anyone better at doing something must have done something that you did not do or have something you do not have. It is possible that they even only have a few things compared to you, but the results they achieved did not require much more than they had, but you did not obtain the same because you had too much of other things but not enough of what the results needed.

You might have heard of so many people investing in shares with the hope to make quick money and double or triple their investment in a short time. Some may have such or even more achievements. Some others lose all they have.

A couple of the small prints I have highlighted with some of those investments are; '…only invest what you can afford to lose.' and '...the price of shares can go up or down, and you could lose all your money.' I have met a few investors that have lost their investment partially or fully at one time or the other. I doubt if anyone exists that has not experienced losses at all and became successful in the trade.

Many do not realise this but copy others expecting the same results. They fail and drown. The more experienced and knowledgeable weather the storm because they have only invested what they could afford to lose or have prepared for the fluctuating prices and are willing to leave their investment to achieve the expected gains after a price rise.

Two investors could invest in the same set of shares but operating at different levels of experiences. They will be obtaining two different results. If you are not prepared to lose, you may not recover when you do. So many people that copy such actions cannot afford to lose at their present level. They have little, they invest all, and expecting it to double, but when the opposite happens, they drown, and things become worse rather than better.

I once heard a property investor that tells his success stories to encourage so many people to invest in property and make lots of money. He had an idea that helped him—it made it more attractive—it was to use other people's money, not your own. It means that he will borrow all the required funds, invest it, make a profit enough to pay back his debt and keep the gains. It sounds good enough to attract anyone interested.

You do not need to have money or use your money. That is a good idea. Right? I soon found from his story that he had lost so many times in the past. He lost all at some point with nothing left. He then said that he turned to his family and friends to help him recover from his loss. He had wealthy people around him that could help him when he falls. He can decide to take high risks that could mean high gains or losses, but those that copy him may not know this, but assume they are all at the same level but not really. The outcome will soon reveal their assumption.

It is easy to get attracted to such testimonies and follow suit. Some may not realise that the people they are copying have some knowledge, support and experiences accumulated over the years that gives them an edge over others. Before you jump, consider where you are—you may not all be jumping from the same platform. The person you decide to copy may have a comfortable support base to cushion the effect of any unpleasant experience.

It is good to desire to improve and become better at what you do. Learning from others can help you in that journey but never forget where you are at the moment. Whoever you desire to be like did not start from their current position. It takes a plan on how to get there from where you are to avoid frustration.

You may want to lose weight, but consider how to start from where you are, gradually working your way to where you desire to be. Rigorous exercises could have helped someone, but they may endanger others because they are not used to such yet. A gradual approach could help get to that point of such levels of activity.

Many great men confirm the importance of time, dedication and focus. Some of those that copy their actions are left frustrated because they cannot cope at their present level and with other commitments. The journey is possible, but it is vital to start from where you are and do what is practicable at that level and gradually move towards your desire.

People tell their stories of success, but unfortunately, you are not them. You need to understand the lessons and see how you can apply them to your life. You may copy the action but never achieve the result because what you are attempting cannot work from where you are.

Many may desire to be Doctors in High School after listening to professionals in the field. They will not be successful if they apply for jobs at that level. They need to understand the level they are at and work towards how to get to their desire. It is wisdom to leave the application for jobs until you are adequately equipped and qualified to do the work. The next thing for the school students will be to prepare for the relevant subjects to gain a university place for their desired course.

If you understand where you are relative to where you are going, you will plan actions that can easily connect you to where you need to be.

Invest your time doing what you need to do from where you are, rather than doing what others are doing from their level. Do not copy all you see without understanding how it applies to you now. It could lead to frustration.

It is possible to be the best, but start from where you are and move forward till you get there. You can learn better from others when you can understand where you are and connect with a plan that helps you apply the lessons as it applies to you from where you are.

CHAPTER 8

Consistency

Many people have desires and expectations that never get fulfilled. They have hopes and dreams that do not come to fruition. Some even criticise others that have better results. They vilify those that have achieved what they are still struggling to attain. They try to reach their goals like others, but it does not work, and they never do.

A lot of people have become what they are today because of what they have done. There could be so many other factors, but chief among them is because of what they have done consistently. It is not what they have done a few times, but what they continued doing.

Many leaders have gained the trust of their followers over the years. They must have shown traits, attributes or character to earn that trust. If they discontinue, it will be lost. The achievement is the effect of doing what they believe and doing so consistently. The confidence of the followers, won by honesty, discipline, integrity, fairness, justice and or dedication, could be lost by acts of dishonesty or a deviation from the values they once upheld.

It is often the case that some forget what made them successful and deviate from such values because of their new status and achievements. They are likely to see their position or achievement lost to someone else that has adopted those values. Many may see such deviations and follow suit but never realise that it leads to a different destination. It is vital to understand that what keeps achievements or success is doing what you need to do consistently.

What often makes people is not what they do some of the time, but what they do all the time. It is what they believe in, so much so that they choose to do it even when it is not convenient.

An American professional boxer, Muhammad Ali, was once asked, 'How many sit-ups do you do per day?' He responded, 'I do not count my sit-ups; I only start counting when it starts hurting because they are the only ones that count.' He was committed to doing exercises daily far beyond comfort until it hurts and then begins to count. If you think of athletes, there will be times they will feel tired, happy, sad, busy, or frustrated. It happens to everyone, but there is a decision to keep on doing it daily regardless of the circumstance because they believe in it and that it is needed to achieve their goal.

It is often easier to achieve any goal than to keep it. Those that maintain that achievement have something in common; it is consistency. It is the power that helps you do what you believe in always even when it hurts. You may not feel like doing those

Consistency

things sometimes, or it could be inconvenient, but you decide to deny yourself the pleasure, compliment, temporary gain so that you can do what you need to do. That is consistency. Keep to it at all times. That is what keeps the achievement.

Many organisations and businesses have seen significant growth by producing quality products and providing excellent customer service consistently. An attempt to deviate from those values will cause a loss of confidence—the trust and loyalty will diminish. The sales may drop, employees may lose their jobs, competitors may take over their customers, and the business may fold up. All these could happen because they refused to continue doing what they once believed. That is why they invest so much in training to keep the values constant in everyone that would be part of the organisation.

John Maxwell once said: 'Small disciplines repeated with consistency every day lead to great achievements gained slowly over time.' If you work hard and keep at it, it will lead to achievements. It is possible for a person with lower potentials but with consistency to do better than one with many with inconsistent attitude.

There was a story of the Hare and the Tortoise. They both participated in a race. The hare was known for speed, while the tortoise for sluggishness. The tortoise decided to participate even though it had no chance of winning but decided to move as fast as it could consistently.

On the other hand, the hare had the potential to win effortlessly. He decided to run ahead of the tortoise but waited to rest when it could not see the tortoise, as it was far behind. The hare slept off in the process, and the sluggish tortoise moved past and won the race.

Many people that are able and mighty lose out in this same manner because of an inconsistent attitude. The tortoise may not always win—in such competitions that match varying strengths, but it could complete the goal set with consistency in its own time.

Do you have people you love and desire to emulate? Find out what their routine looks like; that may be the clue to what you need to start doing immediately and consistently.

The Chinese bamboo tree has an interesting pattern of growth. It is just like any other plant that needs water in addition to sunshine and fertile soil on which it grows. The plant does not show signs of growth in the first four years of consistent nurturing and caring.

The plant grows above the soil in the fifth year to a height of ninety feet in six weeks. The plant was growing daily by the consistent watering and nurturing, but it was growing roots that will support its future growth. It was unseen, but if the farmer did not continue watering, the plant would die.

I found the same to be true of people. Many people we see have invested so much consistently for years, growing a base or foundation to support greatness, but many that copy cannot see the four years of consistent efforts. They only see the six weeks of remarkable growth.

It is crucial to commit to consistency because every success that will last must have the same commitment. There are many great stories of people that have been consistent in honesty, dedication, justice, fairness, integrity, obedience, love, morality, and so on. They chose to be, even in periods of hard times, failures, delays, disappointments, ridicules, ingratitudes, pains, betrayals, among others. Keep on doing what you need to do. You will soon see your bamboo tree emerge.

It is lovely to dream big but do not stop at a desire to be like others. Start by a desire to do what they have done consistently and be willing to do the same. If you do what makes for greatness as part

Consistency

of your routine, even if you do not desire it, you cannot help it because you have committed to a process that takes you to a great destination. You will wake up to discover that you are there.

CHAPTER 9
The Fact

There are so many things that affect the decisions we make and how we see certain situations. You may have been in a circumstance where you knew what was right for you at the time, but you changed your choice because of some other considerations. It could be an influential factor for some people as they may be willing to follow a certain way based on connections, feelings, how they think about others, but not based on facts. It usually occurs when the attachment is more important than the truth.

Many have chosen to follow a lifestyle that they cannot afford. It could be in a bid to please others or be like some people to which they have some attachment. This type of choice is usually an attempt to look or be like some people. It is an attempt to show a false or inflated status than the reality. Some derive happiness from this. Many try so hard to please others and displease themselves in the process. They prefer to destroy themselves so that others may feel they are doing well, even though they are not.

I know a few people that prefer to run their business at a loss. They continue to do so because they want to keep the status of a business owner or Director. They will not accept doing something else that could be profitable but will not have such titles. They try to attract the same honour or respect as some people in the industry, but they are not the same in reality. It could be a gradual decline in some cases, such that they continue to accumulate debts, losing their valuables but will not consider a practical solution to progress. They often make things worse by such an attitude to life.

Some may borrow money to finance birthday parties to give an impression of a similar or higher standard to some of their friends. Many buy cars that affects their finances as the purchase and maintenance cost is far too high than what they could conveniently afford. The only reason why they will not stop and consider the facts is that there is something more important to them than reason, which is to give others a false impression of who they are.

It is the reason why some people buy what they do not need. The only justification is that someone has got it, and since they have some attachment to that person, they also need to get it even when they do not need it and cannot afford it.

There are so many people struggling financially today because of the way they think and make decisions. They spend so much expecting to gain respect from people by being what they are not, but eventually, they discover that it is hard to maintain—it leads them to frustrations. The bid to earn the respect someone has without actually being them or someone like them will lead to disappointment because the truth will reveal the situation with time.

Many follow the errors of their leaders. It is not because they do not know, but because the attachment is more important in their view—they become blind to the mistakes. In places where truth is valued, you will observe that even though a leader is respected, it does not overwrite the wrong. That is why some leaders step down, resign or apologise so that his errors are not approved or seen as something to copy, even if it was from a high profile figure in the society. If the fear of losing the leader is more important than the truth, that community will start to crumble.

So many people have followed leaders they consider to be good. They also sometimes copy their errors because of sentiments even when the facts are there to prove the error. There will always be a problem if we do not face the issues or facts but only make decisions based on sentiments. Everyone should be able to make decisions based on facts, to avoid being misled or creating further problems. You may have witnessed some followers justify every act of their leaders, even when some of them are wrong. They have made the person more important than the facts. It will eventually affect the value of such people.

I once heard a student applying for a Course in the University because a friend chose the Course. The decision may lead her to a different destination because it based on friendship and not facts. The fact that they are friends does not mean they have to make the same choices in life. They are still unique individuals, and each could find fulfilment in different professions. The decision, which may well be the same, could have been made based on facts. It will ensure that they can continue with their lives even if the friendship comes to an end.

A Human resource manager may decide to hire someone incompetent for so many reasons. It may be because they think the same way, look the same, have some attachment, easy to manage, or related. The decision may bring some benefits to the Manager to fulfil some selfish needs. However, it may affect the organisation as the person with the required competence for some reasons was rejected. The business will struggle for the lack of it.

Many people follow this example and put themselves first and watch the whole organisation, community, or nation suffer for such decisions. So many businesses, institutions, and countries have suffered from the effects of such selfish appointments. It is all about sentiments.

There could be times when such decisions may not affect other people, and some might decide to ignore the facts and follow the sentiments for personal reasons. For instance, a situation where a family member is willing to pay more for something that belongs to a loved one. There could be so many things we value because of our attachment to it, and we have the power of choice.

There are so many things people do. We must be careful and study the facts before we make decisions to follow suit. We must also understand the decisions we make and the implications of such, not just on ourselves but others as well.

Many have chosen to follow a lifestyle that they cannot afford. It could be in a bid to please others or be like some people to which they have some attachment.

CHAPTER 10

The Purpose

Have you ever wondered why some people are often satisfied doing what others do and never attempt to check if it is the right thing to do? Have you met with people committed to doing what others have done but do not know the purpose of the actions?

It is common to see many that have kept traditions and passed on the same to others. They have also kept it and passed it on. However, in some cases, some things were lost in such a continuous transition. One of which is the original purpose of such actions. They passed on the activities but not the reasons behind them. It explains the frustration of some people today. They attempt to act like others but do not understand the reasons behind their decisions or actions. It eventually leads to frustration.

Some people are happy to follow a particular way of life, as long as it is accepted by many. It is interesting to see what many people do around the world today. Some people might have seen it as a norm, but that may not necessarily make it so. Sometimes it could be assumptions that have been left unchallenged.

The recommended use of any product implies using it for the purpose stated by the manufacturer. It is following the recommended guidelines, which is a reflection of the purpose for making it. If you decide to use it for any other purpose or outside the recommended guidelines, it is abnormal use or abuse.

It is easy to abuse when the purpose of a thing or person is not known. If you want to find out, it is the answer to the question why. Why do you do what you do? Why do you follow the actions of others? Is it because of what they have said, or you have taken time to discover the purpose of that thing you are doing? If you do what others do and do not know the reason, you may be abusing without knowing.

I was touched by the story of a young man recently that was arrested and jailed for murder. He recalled his relationship with his parents—he was beaten and punished for his misbehaviour. He heard these words every time it happened; 'It hurts me more than it hurts you, but I have to inflict this pain on you because I love you...' He heard those words and concluded that: 'You inflict pain on those you love.'

He grew up with this understanding and inflicted pain on anyone he loves, causing havoc everywhere till he finally murdered a mother and her daughter. He thought torment meant love. His parents did it, but he did not understand the purpose or what they wanted to achieve. He decided to follow suit creating pain everywhere he went. He copied the action but did not understand the reason. Many families have been reduced to tears because they have copied something similar. They want to achieve discipline, but they ended up with tragedy.

There is a difference between punishment and discipline. The goal of the former is pain, while that of the latter is correction and change. It is for a lesson to be learnt and restoration of character. If the reason is not understood, the result will be destructive.

There are so many things in our world today that is known more for their detrimental use than beneficial use. The word cocaine is best known for its abuse on the streets. It is remembered widely for the dreadful repercussions of addiction to such a drug. It is true, but it does have a beneficial purpose. It has legitimate and helpful uses in medicine for anaesthesia and vasoconstriction of the upper respiratory tract.[1] If you do not know, do not copy others to abuse it. It is better to leave it alone than to use it for the wrong reasons.

Many never know the recommended use; they only know the abnormal use because it is popular. It may be seen as or accepted as the norm, but it is not normal. If you do not understand the purpose of anything, you are likely to abuse it. If you do not know the purpose of a drug, you are likely to abuse it. It is called Drug abuse. If you do not understand the purpose of a child, you are likely to abuse the child. It is known as child abuse.

Some do not know the purpose of a parent; they turn them into slaves, that is parent abuse. Many do not understand the purpose of a secretary; they turn them to mistresses or means of pleasure. It is abuse. You must have heard of leaders that have taken advantage of their followers for gain and gratification. They do not understand the purpose of leadership. It is abuse. The news have reported teachers that have engaged in immorality with their students.

The Purpose

It is worrying that some are just teenagers, expecting guidance, but they are misguided.[2] They abused them because they did not understand the purpose of their role.

Those in position of authority are there for a purpose. When there is gross misconduct, it is called abuse of position or power. When the purpose of the law is not known, abuse is the result. The lawmakers can make laws for personal gain or to reward evil and frustrate good. It is abuse.

If you do not understand the purpose of freedom of speech, you will abuse it.

There are some times you may not find the purpose of a thing easily from people around you. The abnormal use may have become popular and accepted, but it does not make it the right choice to follow. You should not join the abusers to continue in the abnormal use. You may need to discover the purpose deliberately. Ask yourself the question Why? What is the purpose of this position? Why this law?

What is the reason for the authority conferred upon me? You can always find out.

Many could be wrong, but if you discover the purpose it could help you make the right decision. There is so much abuse in our world because we do not ask why. The majority follow without asking questions or understanding the purpose.

Wherever you are, you might have become used to some things because everyone does it. It does not make it right. Discover the purpose before you follow suit. Abuse is destructive; even when you think you have some pleasure, it is temporary. There may be some terrible consequences afterwards, which could affect you and the lives of others as well.

The Purpose

If you do what others do and do not know the reason, you may be abusing without knowing.

CHAPTER 11
The Inverse

Information has the potential to influence. It can bring about change in thinking, action or reaction. The giver and the receiver have a significant role to play in the type of change that occurs. They both make decisions, but how do we react to the information we receive?

Every relationship or experience in life allows us to give or receive information—to teach or learn. A teacher provides a lesson with examples to students to encourage them to do the same. The teacher attends the class prepared with examples, showing the advantages of doing it. The aim is to help the students through the benefits to make that choice.

The Inverse

Another teacher may provide a contradictory example—one that negates the opinion, showing the disadvantages. The intention is to help the students see the dangers and avoid that choice. It is to help them choose to do the inverse or the opposite.

Some may choose because of the benefits; others perhaps because of the consequences of doing the inverse. Students usually change their views based on many things, including the teacher, the information they receive, and the level of persuasion.

The same is true for many today in life. We all meet different people in life—some are like the teacher that gives us information. The example, people or experience may not necessarily be for us to copy or follow. It might be an opportunity to see the consequences and choose the inverse.

Moreover, some people provide us with lessons from their imperfections, errors, or failures. We can learn from those too. We not only benefit from those experiences, but they can also benefit from it by changing to get a better result. Many more people could get help to avoid such pitfalls in future if they know better in advance.

You may have observed that some people only want to listen to the great stories or people they consider wise. It is a good idea to follow excellent examples. However, it is also possible to learn from the errors and failures of people too. The 'perfect' professional today was once an amateur. One that probably struggled through different challenges before becoming what you see today. You may find it difficult to see such traces of weakness because it has turned to strength with time, but you can easily relate to those facing such challenges and learn from them.

The consequences of the decisions of some people may help you make a better decision. Someone may have acted foolishly at some point in life—it may have caused great harm or damage to the individual and the community—it could help many others avoid such ways and decide not to follow suit. It could help you get the lesson out of a bad situation or sieve the sense out of non-sense.

The knowledge of what to do is as crucial as what not to do. Doing what you should not do could ruin what you have done.

We can help many people that are frustrated in a continuous loop of errors. It could be beneficial in providing solutions to the challenges that many people face, as they may not realise the reason for their failures.

You can turn the situation around and learn from it by avoiding what led to the error and doing what will lead to a beneficial result.

There is always an opportunity to learn from people. It could be either something to follow or something to avoid. Sometimes we neglect some opportunities because we do not know what the outcome may be.

Some people have already made those mistakes, and they have results to show for it. We can learn from those by avoiding the errors they have once made.

In managing a project, there is often documentation of the knowledge gained, which combines positive and negative experiences. It is known as lessons learnt. It is a vital document, especially after the project, as it provides a knowledge bank for better performance in the future. The negatives help avoid the re-occurrence of any unpleasant event, while the positives give you an indication of what you can replicate.

Many people have surpassed the records in their profession. They achieved the feats, among other things, by learning from the errors of those that have gone ahead and avoiding them. Some have done worse because they repeated the mistakes or multiplied them.

There was once an entrepreneur that was reselling products of a big company.

She gathered interests from her network and had a list of products they would like. She then borrowed money to order the products. She thought those that signified interest would buy it. It was not as she thought—they did to commit or complete the purchase. She had to bear the loss, unfortunately, and it dashed her hope.

Some people have had similar experiences in business, and many have learnt from this mistake. You will often find that some people guarantee commitment or payment from a potential customer. They preserve their time, energy and resources by doing so. Interest in a product is good, but it does mean they will commit to buy.

In one of the national election years, the party in power had the lead in the opinion polls. As we counted down towards the election, the victory seemed inevitable. The party took advantage of this to make changes that affected some people—they eventually changed their decision. The party did not win as expected and ended up in a coalition government without the majority required, which led to frustration and another election.[1] The new leader learnt from the mistakes and achieved victory with record majority seats in the next election. It was the biggest majority win for the preceding thirty-two years.[2] Some leaders have lost their position similarly because of some mistakes they made during their term in office. Some have learnt, avoided those errors and have been able to achieve a better result; some have unfortunately followed suit and ended up in even worse situations.

I know of people that lend money or offer services without any formal agreement or documentation. It later led to arguments and eventually loss of the funds or income. Many have learnt from this and implemented necessary agreement to avoid such disagreements and losses.

There have been disputes that led to chaos in some organisations because of the lack of documented policy. A policy, well written, understandable and accessible, has saved such commotion when implemented in an organisation, community or nation. Some learnt from the mistakes and provided solutions to avoid a repeat.

We can learn more from errors because it can help achieve and maintain a better result. You can always ask yourself the following questions when you come across such an opportunity: What can I learn from this mistake? What can I do to achieve a better result? How can this consequence be avoided? You will be helping not just yourself but those having such challenges and many that are likely to fall into the same trap in the future.

Learn a lesson from the mistake of others and proffer an action that will improve the result. Be careful not to follow the errors but learn from them and do the inverse.

CHAPTER 12

The Action

Have you ever thought of what makes people who they are? What do you think might be responsible for some of the traits you see in people? What are the factors that delivered the achievements you desire in others? Do you know why two people with the same opportunities end up with different results? It is what we choose to do, and by implication, what we have refused to do.

Everyone is a product of their actions. We are what we are today because of what we did or did not do yesterday. A doctor today was a student that chose a particular path of study, a specific career path, and willingly subjected to the disciplines required till the dream came to reality.

The Action

Everybody could be a doctor, or at least, everyone has that potential, but why is everyone not a doctor? It is simple. It is because the others have chosen a different path that leads to something else.

Doctors have some privileges. They have uniforms and some other essentials peculiar to the profession, like a stethoscope. All these are essential because of the individual's actions that had led to being a qualified medical professional. It will not be relevant to another professional in a different discipline.

There are some necessities for the job, which helps them do what they have trained to do. There are also privileges they enjoy because of what they do to those affected by their service. When medical students qualify as medical doctors, they can place the title 'Dr.' before their names. They have uniforms, accessories, amongst others, related to their job. It is the result of the process followed. The individual is a doctor, so he is entitled to those things, and anyone that follows the same path could enjoy the same.

The result is not the action. If you want the same, you have to follow the same process. You could copy the uniform—buy and wear the same, but that does not make you a doctor—following the same path does. Can you imagine someone using the prefix Dr before his/her name, wearing the same uniform with a stethoscope around the neck? It is possible, but that does not make him/her a doctor—it is self-deceit. You cannot copy the result and be genuine. You can only follow the process to get the results. You should not copy the uniforms but copy the actions that led to the results to get the same outcome.

Some people buy the same brands, like some rich people, even though they cannot afford it without borrowing. They hope that they will get the same honour and influence by copying their results and ignoring the actions that led to it. If you buy the same car as the rich, it does not make you rich. If

The Action

you wear the same wristwatch as the King, that does not make you influential. Wearing a well-designed wig does not make you a lawyer. An expensive stethoscope around your neck does not make you a doctor. Drinking tea in a hotel lounge with a suit and tie does not make you a CEO. What makes you one is doing the actions and following the same process.

A lot of people are only attracted by the result and ignore the actions. Some have a good knowledge of the required steps to get to where they desire to be but have had so many excuses of not following that path, but rather prefer to continue wasting their time posing with the results with no evidence to show. They say, 'you can fake it until you make it' instead of saying; if you want to get what he got, do what he did.

Many people that have achieved their goals have many things in common. If you study some, you will find out that there are similarities in every success story. If you also want to join that company of fulfilled people, you must be determined to do the same concerning your goals and assignment.

There is a price to pay, there is time to be invested, there are things to be denied, there is a lifestyle that you have to conform to, and there are changes required. If what you are doing is not getting you closer to what you desire, it may be a clue that you are doing something wrong. Find out and be willing to make the change.

Can you put in the same hours as some of the athletes do? Can you work as hard as some of the CEOs? Can you exercise the same level of discipline as some of those leaders? Can you deny yourself like some of those inventors? Can you be as focused as some of those pacesetters? Can you endure pain like some of those entrepreneurs?

Can you be as selfless as that spouse? Can you be as dedicated as that first class student? Can you be as loving as those parents? Can you accept loss like some of those organisations? Can you withstand such discipline as some of the military personnel do? They enjoy the benefits of what they have done—you can also benefit from the same if you are willing to do likewise.

Many people do not realise that many fulfilled goals were due to the willingness to do more than was required. It is often tough choices. The choice to swim against the current; willing to do what others do not want to do, willing to sacrifice, and happy to keep to their values even when it hurts. It is hard work. It is the price the successful are willing to pay.

It is good practice to ask yourself the following questions when you see the results of others. What did my friend do to achieve the result? Which path has she taken? How did he arrive at this destination or become what she is today? What is his history? What is her story? Can I do the same? If you can follow the action, you get the same outcome.

You will always find out that the outcome was due to an input that someone was willing to do. It is because of a price someone was happy to pay. Instead of faking it, try to understand what they have done to get to where they are and be willing to pay the price to do the same if you desire the same result. Be careful to follow the actions and process and not copy the results in self-deceit.

If what you are doing is not getting you closer to what you desire, it may be a clue that you are doing something wrong. Find out and be willing to make the change.

CHAPTER 13

The Priorities

Have you ever witnessed a dispute between students over their performance, especially when one thinks he should have a better result or grade than another student? Have you ever felt you could not learn from another person because of some of the errors or mistakes they have made? Have you ever thought that you deserve more, and another person should have had less? You are not alone; many share similar experiences in our world today.

It is interesting how life works, and also how many people are ignorant of how things work. One of the vital school lessons is the understanding of the grading system. It is an insight into the method of assessment for the course you have chosen

The Priorities

to study. The information is available as early as possible before any work, test, project or action—right or wrong, is assessed to ensure everyone is starting from the same fresh slate with the same opportunities.

It usually states courses and their level of importance, with some compulsory, some electives and in some cases, some do not even have any score—they are just for information. They also explain how each score translates to a final grade. It helps students prepare and prioritise their actions, but many people neglect, trivialise or reject this to suffer the consequences afterwards.

There are different grading systems used in various countries, but there is something similar to most, if not, all of them. It is the fact that a range of marks represents a grade. For instance, in the UK, you will be awarded the highest possible class if you score between 70 and 100 inclusive. Typically, 60 to 69 form a lower grade, followed by scores from 50 to 59. The scores 40 to 49 represent the next lower category. The scores below this score bracket represent a fail.

Any score within the range has the same grade, and one score below the minimum drops you to a lower class. A score of 69 could be a second class, while 70, 71, 99 or 100 is still a first-class. You may understand the feeling of a student that lost a higher grade by one score. You may probably relate to the frustration of another that could not improve his class—even though he has nine scores above the minimum required.

It also implies that the best student in a particular discipline does not need to score a hundred to secure a place in the best category. He does not need to know everything; he does not need to be perfect. He needs to know at least 70% of the relevant things to be graded as such. Those that failed may have a better knowledge of so many others things and probably do well in many other things, but they are graded as failures because they do not have the relevant marks required by the course of study to be in the category of those that have passed. The system rewards only those whose priorities match those set by the institution. If the compulsory course is not vital to you—no matter how brilliant you are in every other subject, failure in the mandatory will automatically make you a failure by the grading system.

It is a vital lesson in life. The best student in the class does not mean the best student in everything or the best student in the world or every area of life. It is the student that best aligns his/her priorities with that of the course.

A Professor of sciences does not mean he knows everything about sciences but enough to earn a degree to practice in the field. He still has faults; he is not an expert in everything. He may have so many things to teach others about sciences, but probably there are some other areas of life that he does not have the relevant knowledge to help anyone.

It is surprising how many people depend on those that could not help them. A mechanic that has done professional work on your car is not the best person for your toothache. A good or diligent man, respected and loved, may not be able to help you when you are in crisis—he may not have what you need. He may be good, diligent and respected, but you need someone with relevant information or skill to solve the problem you have.

Many people excel and become experts by getting their priorities right, focusing on the critical things to achieving their goal. If you know the core part of the course and devote the necessary time and focus, you can earn a good grade. It implies that you may have neglected some other things to achieve this one goal. It all depends on what is important to you.

Some other people may have different or more priorities and would have done well in many of those areas instead of achieving excellence in one at the expense of so many others.

You may have heard of stories of children that pass their A level test at a very young age or one that completed a professional examination while in primary school. Some mastered a music instrument or a game better than a professional or got the highest grade possible in a subject at a young age, of say nine. It is not a lie, neither is it necessarily exceptional. It simply an issue of priority. A child can become an expert if ninety per cent of his time goes to that one thing, but it only means some others areas of his life will suffer for lack of time and development. It depends on what is most important.

A couple with children may not be willing to sacrifice family time to achieve only one goal. They could manage their priorities to ensure they do not achieve one great success with an adverse effect on their family. We often neglect this factor when we compare or copy others. We may not have the same priorities, or we may not understand the grading systems well enough to do what is required to excel.

Many cannot come to terms with the success of some people. They have done what is required to excel in their field. Some may focus on their weakness, but they have done well regardless of that. They understood the system and aligned their priorities accordingly. Bill Gates and Mark Zuckerberg left Harvard to focus on something more vital to them. The degree was not the most important to them but a future they are capable of building. They opened the world to great opportunities because they have done what is more important to them and excelled. Sometimes some people neglect one thing so that they can achieve another, it may seem they have failed in one, but it is because it was less important to them than some others.

You may have wondered why a manufacturer will be happy to lose when a

The Priorities

customer is not happy with the purchase. They prefer to replace the item at a loss to the company. It is because the satisfaction of the customer is more important. To protect the name or brand is a higher priority. It may not be the best economic strategy for maximising profits, but something is more important than the profit that the manufacturer would prefer to succeed in.

Many have succeeded in one area of life at the expense of so many other areas of their life. Some have done well professionally, but their health, social life, relationships, family, or other areas that could affect their lives, suffered adversely.

A few have focused so much on making money but neglected the wellbeing and development of their children. They succeed in one aspect, but the failure in one neglected area robbed them of the joy. Some have made financial fortunes by taking advantage of the vulnerable—gain was more important, but they failed to realise that they have sown an evil seed that will yield corresponding fruits.

It is good practice to evaluate your priorities and ensure they reflect what you desire to achieve. Ask yourself sincere questions before you do what others are doing. What is the most important thing to me, and what do I need to do to fulfil it? Will I neglect my priorities by doing this? Is this in line with what I consider vital? Will this cost me by damaging what I value? Does this reflect my values? Will I achieve this at the detriment of something critical to my future or that of others? Be sincere and truthful. Choose right.

The people you desire to follow may be behaving the way they are because of what is uppermost on their list. Set yours, look for what you need, do not focus on others, stick to what is most important to you. Set your priorities right.

Many people excel and become experts by getting their priorities right, focusing on the critical things to achieving their goal.

CHAPTER 14

Cumulative Actions

It was an old metal pole that has become a nuisance, and everyone in the community wanted to get rid of it. Only if it were that easy—it would have been uprooted by the first person at the first attempt. Not so—many people had their fair try and gave up trying again later, while some never again.

A Push, a pull and all sorts of forces, applied to get the pole out of the way. It seems not to give way. Everyone tried, exerted some effort and went away after a while as it did not give way. The bound was not as strong after each attempt, but it did not collapse. One day, a young boy came around, having another chance to pull, and in a couple of tries, brought it down. Hurray! He shouted—I did it. He brought it

Cumulative Actions

down. Did he? How many people do you think brought the pole down? The efforts of everyone before him contributed to the weakening of the bound that caused it to collapse.

You might have witnessed the result of the hard work of friends or colleagues presented, and you think, 'That is great, but I can do the same, even better.' A Student may comment about a group project and say, 'I got it, it is easy, I can do it easily.' The experience may be different.

Have you ever witnessed the cleaning of a heavily stained surface? Initially, you may have thought it could not be that hard but changed your mind afterwards when you observed the process. You may have found it to be true. There is usually a change of mind when the details are known.

An adventurer once decided to cut a giant pine tree with an axe. He started the task and was committed to it. He hit the tree hard with the axe and continued until the axe head fell off. He was determined to finish up the task, so he sought a suitable log to hold the axe head in place. The makeshift solution worked, so he was able to continue the cutting of the tree. He paused to rest when he was tired and also to sharpen his tool. He continued with dedication for over three hours.

He cut deep into a depth of about 80% of the diameter of the tree. He had by this time carved a notch out of the side of the tree. It was facing the felling direction. After some rest, he decided to call some friends to witness the final part as he knows the task is near completion.

They gathered as he puts in his last efforts, striking the tree from the opposite side a few times. He struck with the axe, not too many times more before the noise of cracking was heard. The tree fell into the river nearby, and the friends applauded the feat. None of them witnessed the beginning; they only saw the ending, which looked easy and effortless.

Cumulative Actions

Some of them judged by the last action, and they went away thinking it was easy, but in reality, it was not as easy as they thought. Three hours of labour have gone into the project already. The tree will not come down with just a few of the final strokes. All the strokes were necessary for the tree to fall.

I found this to be also true in life. We are often only invited to graduation ceremonies, commissioning ceremonies, launching ceremonies, presentations and so on, but that does not give us a picture of the hours of labour invested. It is deceit to believe that there is nothing more that is required. There is, all the actions added up to produce success in the end.

Sometimes we neglect some factors that contribute to success. One of them is the power of cumulative action. The last activity is crucial for completion. However, If there were no prior efforts, the final one will not be the concluding action. Every one of them is necessary to get the job done—none should be ignored or neglected.

A doctor may pass a professional exam in his field by preparing for it within six hours and probably registering to sit it within two weeks. He could achieve it not only because of the six hours of preparation but also all the relevant cumulative learning in all schools attended, college and university. If you attempt to do the same, coming from a dissimilar background or with less experience, and only prepare for six hours, you may not pass, let alone get the same result.

You may have attempted to collapse a wooden barrier or fence. You may have found that every effort weakens the wood but may not break it. It will eventually collapse, but the last action and the others before it will contribute to the result.

Many succeed in business, not just because they have a product; cumulative learning through experiences and research must have contributed to their success.

Cumulative Actions

Many fail because they start to copy from the end and never knew there was a beginning, which, unfortunately, many people would not advertise anyway. Many have copied successful people by only doing a few of their actions and expecting the same result. There is more in their story—you can only understand if you start from the beginning.

I have heard of people that turn up to learn a new business or skill and only get some final tips and ideas. They ask a few questions, and they seem to have gotten it all and know what to do from beginning to the end. It does not always work like that. They soon find that when they try to do it, they encounter problems—it is not as easy as it seems. They have lost the three hours of labour and struggling to replicate and make sense of the success that happened within the final five minutes.

Life is not always as it seems. There could be more to what you are seeing than meets the eyes. If you desire the same result, you should be willing to study the whole process. It is not just one action—it is all the actions that make it work.

You may be underestimating the cumulative actions of others on the achievements you see. It may imply that you are missing out on the whole picture or reality of things. It is better to make decisions based on facts than assumptions. You may have been trying only the last set of actions, which may explain why the result is not as you expected.

The seemingly effortless success we see is due to the various contributions of people. They have made the necessary preliminary actions that made it easy for a simple effort to bring out the result. It may be worth considering a holistic approach to see what others may have contributed to the outcome.

You may be on the right track but probably need encouragement to continue. Do not give up. Those that are celebrating today must have started sometime in the past. If you continue on the right track, you will soon get to the finish line and have cause for celebration. It is not just the last one, but the combination of all the actions that count.

CHAPTER 15

The Multitudes

There are so many things that influence the decisions people make. One of them is the decision of other people. You may have witnessed a situation where people ask others about their choice before they make theirs. Their choice depends solely on other people.

It could be by way of asking questions like; Which option did you choose?—they follow the same—Who did you vote for in the election?—the same becomes their choice—Which one is the most popular?—if it is popular, it is the best—Which one would you buy?—buying the same is a good idea—What would you do?—doing the same is the best option—Which one do most people like?—it will be good for me.

The Multitudes

Some people may ask such questions to make informed choices, but for some others, it is to follow the popular decision—if it is good for them, it is the best for me.

You have probably seen commuters choose a busy line in the train station without ascertaining if it were the right one for them. You may have witnessed diners opt for the popular menu in the restaurant. They do not see the need to check if there are options that closely suits their requirements. It may be a career choice, without a sound knowledge of where it would lead or an investment in a business venture without relevant information on how to run it. The only reason for doing it is that someone else is doing it.

There are so many ways people decide which way to go or what to choose. One of them is by going with the majority. It is choosing to go with the multitude. It is typically following what other people do without any persuasion. They usually see life as a game of numbers, where the winning team is the one with the most people.

They know right and wrong by the number or the calibre of people doing it. It is accepted as right when the majority is in agreement and wrong when the minority disagrees. The decision is based on the numbers and not the truth. The game of numbers has robbed many of their future.

Many have accepted to stoop so low as to follow without seemingly thinking of their decisions or the implications. They only follow the steps of the influential and take it as a standard. Most often than not, they follow in error and face the consequences. There are times in life where the best thing for you to do is to flow against the current like a fish. Those that stand out from the crowd will need to do something different from the multitude.

A Dutch philosopher and scholar, Desiderius Erasmus, once said, 'In the kingdom of the blind, the one-eyed man is king.' Can you imagine a kingdom where everyone is blind except one with one eye? The majority is blind, and they have probably accepted that 'if there is a man with one eye, he is the greatest, and we should follow him in everything.'

Some people act this way. They will usually put themselves at the mercy of others. There are so many reasons for this type of behaviour. It could be because they do not know or do not have as much as the other person. If you can see, those that cannot see will follow you. If you agree that you cannot, you will follow the multitude and act as if you have lost your sight. The one-eyed man could have decided to follow the crowd as well, but he decided not to, even though he is the only one different.

One thousand people ignorant of technology can be easily deceived by one with a vague idea of the subject. They will all probably agree because they do not know any better. We must desire to improve the power to make the right choices. We can acquire more information, compare facts, verify sources, confirm the truth, search and check the details for credibility. The decision of another person may not be the best for you. It may not be appropriate.

It is worth investing time in the decisions that you make. If you do not, you will remain in darkness and led by those with any form of light.

More does not always mean right, and the fact that you lack does not mean you should agree with everything that comes your way from those that have what you lack. The ability you have seen in them is probably valued because it is the only one prevalent. It could be because others have not realised what it takes or prefer to follow those that have it regardless of whether it is right or wrong.

If all but a few people in a community think the same way, they are likely to win because they are more, but that does not mean they are right. If they get more enlightened, the views of the few may become widely accepted.

The sale of materials at auctions could be sometimes unpredictable. They often have a price range estimated by valuers for such items, but there have been many instances of surprises. Yes, cases where the items sell exceedingly above the estimated or ridiculously below the expected price. There is a power that drives the price; it is the power of the numbers of those interested. It could be a useless item, but if more people show interest in it or the rich and influential have some sentimental value for it, in such situations, trash becomes gold. However, gold becomes trash if the reverse is the case. It is the game of numbers— the power of prevalence.

If you have not been able to make your own decisions, it might be because you do not have enough information, skills, expertise or ability to do so. You could challenge yourself to self-development to equip yourself to make informed decisions rather than going with the multitude. It could be painful to follow the popular path to discover that you have missed the right track.

You may have followed others blindly and are suffering as a result. It may be time to stop and think. It may be a turning point for you. Be involved in the decision-making process of your life. Do not let it be the crowd that controls what you do or not do. They may not always be wrong, but they may not be right all the time either. It is your responsibility to ensure you have enough information to make the right decisions at all times.

Now is the time for a change if you have not done so already. The time to get the facts right, the details straight, and search for knowledge so that you can see, is now. Do not follow the crowd because many could be wrong. Be happy to stand alone if need be and follow the right path based on an informed decision. Dare to be different.

It is worth investing time in the decisions that you make. If you do not, you will remain in darkness and led by those with any form of light.

CHAPTER 16

The Responsibility

You may have met people that blame others for every unpleasant thing that happens to them? They say, 'It is your fault.' Yes, you may have heard some people blame others for their misfortune and credit themselves for their fortunes even though in both cases they learnt from other people.

A mentor once taught his followers about investment, and he got most of them to follow what he did. He made a lot of money and multiplied his initial investment in a short time. Many copied his actions expecting the same, but unfortunately, it did not turn out as expected, so they experienced losses instead of profits. The next thing for most of them was to blame the mentor for their misfortune. He made

The Responsibility

us lose; he ruined our lives—a typical response.

What do you think their reactions would have been if they all made the same level of gains or more? It is usually common to see people blame others for what has happened to them, but they seem to do so only when things go wrong. They are happy to take the praise when things turn out well, more often than not.

If you decide to copy others, your actions become your responsibility. The outcome of your actions also becomes your responsibility. If you are not sure of the activities or the corresponding result, you should do your research. You need to be aware of the implications of what you are doing. There are so many unpleasant experiences that have robbed many of their hard-earned money. Some have learnt from it and have provided some information to help others in the same position. It appears in the small prints or caveat in some cases. The idea is that whatsoever you have chosen to do with your money is your choice. You cannot hold us responsible for your results. You are responsible for your actions and outcomes. You can learn as much as you desire from anyone, but you will be held accountable for what you decide to do.

You may have heard of Ponzi schemes—it is a form of fraud that entices investors. It usually depends on personal networks for advertisement. The earlier investors take profits which they reveal to would-be investors. It serves as an attraction to encourage them to invest in the same—to cash in on similar profits.

The initial payments to the earlier investors usually come from the funds from the recent investors. As the scheme progresses, a time comes when the former boast of gains while the latter can no longer get their investment less alone profits. A seemingly lucrative investment opportunity for one has become a total loss for another. Many people have lost a significant amount of money by following some get-rich-quick schemes like this. They copied others without knowing what they were getting into and ended up robbed.

They probably got enticed by quick and easy profits or did not know enough and trusted someone else instead of taking responsibility themselves. They lost all instead of making the anticipated profit. You should own your decisions and the corresponding outcome. If you can blame others for failing, you should probably blame others for your success as well, because it was perhaps not your own decision but that of someone else.

If the scheme looks fraudulent or otherwise, and you decide to participate, it is your decision, and you should be happy to take the blame or praise for whatever comes as a result. Everyone has a free will to make the right choices. If they have refused to participate after careful research, they would have saved themselves the trouble. If you decide to copy, it is your responsibility to make sure you understand and are happy with what you are doing.

A business that offers profits without a clear understanding of how they make money could be suspicious. A choice to follow without finding out may lead to trouble which would make you liable. It is like going deliberately against the law. Anytime you follow others to do so because the profits are enticing or because you have not found out what they do, that reason will not exempt you. If you decide to copy, it is your responsibility.

Some people might be frustrated because of one choice or the other in their career, family, finances, or other areas of their lives. They probably copied others, but they never got to the end they expected—the journey was not as it seemed. They are stranded because they never owned the decision or understood what they were doing. They were following what others were doing or saying. The time for anyone

The Responsibility

in such circumstance to take ownership is now. It is vital to stop and think. It is crucial to turn in the right direction.

You are where you are today because of what you chose to do yesterday. You would be in a different place tomorrow based on what you decide to do today. The control belongs to you, so do not give it to another person.

Be careful who you follow or copy. A wrong choice could mean loss, and a right one could translate to gain and peace of mind. It all depends on you. Whichever way you follow, you are the first to blame because you agreed to follow. It is your responsibility, so take responsibility for the things you do and what happens afterwards.

Have you followed someone in error and found that you are not where you expected? Have you patterned your life in a certain way and discovered it was not worth it? Take responsibility for your actions and retrace your steps to begin on the right track. You will probably be excited if the ending was great. You will smile and accept the praise. If it has gone wrong, do not blame anyone—own your decision and initiate a change for the better. It is your responsibility, not theirs.

The Responsibility

Be careful who you follow or copy. A wrong choice could mean loss, and a right one could translate to gain and peace of mind. It all depends on you.

CHAPTER 17
Know or Do?

Enriched with the ability to transform anyone that applies it judiciously, information is one of the most sought commodities in the world today. People get it for various reasons; some people desire to put it to use but encounter frustration and disappointments. It is one of the most frustrating experiences in life—failing to achieve the desired outcome.

Have you ever wondered why some people find it difficult to replicate their desired result? Do you know why some are frustrated in an attempt to do what they have heard?

It is interesting to know that there are numerous sources, so many people in the world to learn from, but different people impart different skills. They may help provide knowledge, but it may not be sufficient to do what we intend to do. Some give you enough to be informed, while others go further to empower you to reproduce the same action. It all depends on what you want.

Let us imagine a young boy that wants to learn how to fish. He gets information about the process in the comfort of his home or classroom from someone with enough knowledge about the process. He follows the lesson and attempts to put to use what he has learnt. He goes fishing and discovers that he could not complete the process. He could say it—information, but he cannot do it. He knows what to expect, but something is missing—how to make it happen. He could carefully explain how to catch a fish, but doing it is an entirely different experience. He learnt, but from someone that only teaches what to do. He is now confronting a situation that demands how to get it done.

Some young adults may attempt their first barbeque after some information about the process. They get all the tools required plus the materials for the event just like those experienced in it will do. They have a good knowledge of how the end product should look, and they have an idea of what to do—all set and ready to go or get the party started—not really, as it is not as easy as it appears. They seem not to achieve the desired result—they get disappointed or frustrated instead.

You may have witnessed some of the signs that follow such adventures, like burnt food, not well-cooked food, many injuries, food with fuel smells, and damaged tools, among others. They got the information, but it was missing so many steps that could enable them to practise. Many people only appreciate a cook that provides a nice meal when they attempt to do the same but discover that it demands more than they imagined. It takes a lot to achieve that level of goodness continually—it is a result of experience.

You may get the same tool or even a better one but end up with a worse result. There is something more than the process or tools they use—it is the experience they have acquired through doing the actions. There are so many things you cannot repeat successfully just by getting information or reading the instructions. You need experience.

A young student once got home to cook after some information about cooking. He placed a plastic container on the cooker to cook his food. He was told to put his food in a container and heat it, but he did not know that plastic, though a container, is not one of those containers that can do that job. It was an unpleasant sight—he could not eat any of it. He would have gained more by learning from someone that cooks, as he would be able to pick up all the details and get real-life experience.

Another student attempted to repeat a baking feat, but it ended up a disaster. She realised that there are so many things she did not know that affected her outcome. She later watched an experienced woman and discovered more details.

The effect of preheating the oven, the importance of the different temperature settings and the significance of the various layers available were some of the discoveries. She concluded that there was more to it than just placing the dough in the oven and turning the knob.

It always looks easy to do when it is said, it seems effortless when the experienced people do it, but an attempt to do it usually exposes gaps that could only get filled by experience. It explains the frustration of many people—they know, but what they know is not sufficient to produce the desired outcome.

Imagine an apprentice that wants to learn how to bake bread. He/she could receive instruction from anyone that has such information. The information could be correct, but there are so many things that will still be required if he/she desires to put the knowledge to use.

Another apprentice that shadows a baker in real life situation would probably have more practical information than the first. He would have more confidence in the process—see how the process works and can see the expected outcome.

If the latter continues to bake under the supervision of the baker, he would be able to master the actual process and produce the same result, gaining skill and expertise through the opportunity to follow the actions of the baker. It soon becomes a skill. It is mastered with time and can produce the same result anywhere.

The former, however, may struggle in a real-life scenario because it would be a new experience for the apprentice. What is the difference between the two? One learnt from someone that knows the other from someone that practises. Many people desire to do or copy other people they see or admire. They end up in frustration because they are learning from those that teach. They never show them how to put the learning to use. They are missing the hands-on skills to put the knowledge to practise. The experience is not there.

A young graduate at the outset of his career followed so many people that acquired knowledge and certifications in Information Technology. The aim was to increase the prospects of getting a lucrative job and be easily singled out of the crowd. It has become a popular trend.

Many people display their certifications everywhere possible, and some as a suffix after their name. The more you have, it seemed, the more acceptable you are. So there has been a continuous chase for certifications.

He attempted so many of them, especially the popular ones. He discovered that although he was learning more and knew more, it was difficult to practise or prove the knowledge because he did not have the hands-on experience or the environment to practise. If you desire to know, learn from teachers, but if you are going further to practise, learn from the practitioners.

There are so many frustrated graduates around the world today. They have good certificates to prove knowledge but cannot function in their field of choice. They desire gainful employment, but the employers need people that can do the work and not those that only gained some knowledge.

I found that most employers seek Engineers that can fix problems. They will hire an Architect that can do the job. The certificate will not add value to the business—they need someone that can produce corresponding results.

I once attended a training session organised by a company to deploy one of their products in our environment. The young man explored the configuration of the product and its benefit on well-designed and informative PowerPoint slides. I felt confident and thought I had enough information to do it myself.

I got back to implement what I have learnt, and I discovered that I could not complete the configuration. I understood all he said, but it was not sufficient for me to do the same. I got stuck and could not go ahead. I had to engage the help of a colleague with practical knowledge that guided me through the actual process and solved the problems encountered in the process.

That is what happens when we learn from those that give information alone and expect to become those that produce or reproduce a product. There are some problems you may encounter in an attempt to do or practise. It is often someone that has gone through it before who can help you resolve it.

You might have attended training sessions, seminars, conferences, exhibitions, and so many other information-gathering sessions and found that it seems good but not that easy to reproduce. You may need to learn more from those that practise and not just those that teach.

You need to decide what you want and understand how to get it. If you only need the information, there are so many information givers. If you desire to produce results with what you know, you may need to learn under those that practise—people that do it so well. You will see the whole process and learn how to do the same and become a doer and not just an accumulator of information.

Have you struggled to put into productive use some of the information you have gathered over the years? It may be time to look for those that practise and be willing to learn from them. If you cannot make it work, it implies that you may not know enough to make it work. Search for doers, so you can learn and become one of them.

If you want to know, learn from those that teach. If you desire to do, learn from those that practise.

If you want to know, learn from those that teach. If you desire to do, learn from those that practise.

CHAPTER 18
I am Surprised

There are so many things that happen in life that are out of our control. We least expect some and never imagine some others would happen. However, there are times that our expectation differs from the actual outcome because we do not understand the concept of cause and effect.

We often show this in our reaction to the result. It becomes very confusing when there is a feeling that something else, usually the opposite, was desired to happen. I wonder what you expect as an outcome of what you do and if it has ever come as a surprise.

You may have observed some expressions that you found astonishing or

I am Surprised

probably some that you wondered why the individual involved was astounded.

Have you ever seen a student depress the buttons displaying 10, +, 10, and = on the calculator keypad and feels stunned that the output is 20? You, probably like me, would have asked the student, 'what were you expecting?' It seems the student was expecting something different. I am surprised because the output is an accurate result as far as mathematics is concerned. Unfortunately, there are so many people around the world that behave similarly. They add the numbers like the student, but they are shocked when they get the answer.

Imagine a factory worker caught stealing. He then looks stupefied. You may then wonder, probably he was expecting a different outcome.

You may have witnessed the shocking look of some employees or meeting attendees—they started their journey late and arrived late for work or the meeting.

The travel will not be quicker under normal circumstances, but they were expecting to be early, even though they started late. I wonder why.

Consider a scenario where you would like to board a train to work or for an appointment—the train company involved has a reliable record of efficiency and promptness. It takes ten minutes to get to the train station, and the next train can take you to your destination on time. It is due to leave in 12 minutes, but you decided to depart for the train station after 3 minutes, and you saw the train depart as you approached the station. You exclaimed, No! It seems that was a surprise—I wonder why.

Some people expect a different result from what their actions could guarantee. They do one thing and hope the outcome will not conform to the known standard or probably be inconsistent with what is right. They wish for the result that comes by doing something different. They sow apple seeds and are surprised to have apple fruits as harvest. They seem to be expecting pineapples from an apple seed. They looked stunned, but I wonder why. I am confused that they are surprised.

I have seen some motorists go over the speed limit regularly and are shocked to get a fine in the post. I am not sure what they were expecting.

There may be a restaurant that serves stale food to diners. Do you think they should be shocked if the customers refuse to turn up again? Can you imagine a supermarket that does not value its customers anymore? Yet, they keep wondering why they are all buying from their competitors. They still expect to maintain the same level of sales as they have done in the past—they cannot connect their actions to the outcome.

It should not be strange to see diminished interest in any business that offers fake or substandard products. Those that have provided substandard services should not expect more patronage. They should know the reason for their experience. It will be strange otherwise.

Politicians that abuse the privilege and trust bestowed by voters should not be sad when the people reject them in the polls. A nation that votes in corrupt leaders should not be agitated when they make bad laws; it should not surprise when they promote injustice. Those that vote to secure their selfish interests should not be alarmed at the consequences of their choices. There is always a corresponding result for every decision. It should not come as a surprise.

I have seen some people that follow their friends to visit expensive stores, restaurants or events. They buy the same things they buy and spend the same way without limit. They soon realise that their bank account has gone red or credit card spent over the limit. Your guess may be as good as mine; they were surprised. It is shocking to see many people that keep spending on anything or everything they see. They are still expecting that their bank accounts will remain full of money. They spend on what they cannot afford to please people that do not care. They still wonder, 'Where did all my money go?' or 'Why was my cheque returned, marked "insufficient funds"?'

You may have heard of a situation where someone gets a 'bargain' on a car or device. He pays a tenth of the original value but later discovered that it has some critical problems and is agitated. He should remember that he paid ninety per cent less than it was worth, so it seems that is the value he got—if it is too cheap, it could be so for a reason. He should not be alarmed.

A student refuses to read the relevant materials for his test and gets a result with a fail, and he wonders why? I am not sure what he is expecting. Success in the test is to show that you understand the material—not that you own it.

I know an employee that often takes time off for pleasure. He gets his paycheck and is amazed—it is too small, it is not enough. I was expecting more than this amount. You may wonder what his expectation was when he refused to work his assigned hours because of fun. I wonder.

Some watch movies all night; they get to work the following day and sleep or dose off in the course of their work. They seem to wonder what is wrong when they get told off or embarrassed. If you do not want a repeat, avoid the action.

A young man drives around town with his friends. One mentions a place, and off they go, moving from one place to another. You then find that he is surprised some days after—he ran out of fuel—his response; I only just filled the tank the other day. He probably expected it to continue to multiply or increase as he drives his friends around town. It does not work that way.

An employee was paid monthly but decided to spend everything in the first week. He keeps buying everything that his eyes can see in the stores, especially those on promotion. He could not get what he needs after some days as he has run out of

I am Surprised

funds. He then checks his account balance every day afterwards—he is probably expecting the money spent to reappear in his account. He has some complaint to make to everyone he meets in the day—I do not have money, I only have a few slices of bread and water left, not even milk to make tea. He is confident and knows how to spend his money, but he is surprised that he does not have anything left. I wonder how that works.

It is like walking in the rain and wondering why you got wet or spreading your clothes in the sun and expecting them to remain wet after some hours. You only need to do the action; the outcome becomes predictable. If you are not sure of the result, you should have exercised caution before committing to the action. If you are happy to act the way you do and are surprised at the outcome, it may be a sign that you do not understand the consequences of your actions. If it does surprise you, it may be worth considering the activities that led to it.

Some may spend little or no time practising or developing their skill—they spend the majority of their time for pleasure and sleep and wonder why they have not mastered the skill. The activities you treasure are delivering their predicted results—you should not be alarmed—you should be otherwise.

If you decide to copy others, expect the same result that they get. If you are in doubt, it is probably worth checking before you copy. Actions produce results. Your expectations will not help change the outcome.

If you sow a blueberry seed, you should not be surprised if you harvest blueberry fruits. It is not strange; that is why I am shocked when people look flabbergasted when they get the result of the seed they have sown—I am surprised that they are astonished.

I am Surprised

I am shocked when people look flabbergasted when they get the result of the seed they have sown—I am surprised that they are astonished.

CHAPTER 19

The Scope

Many things in life frustrate us, many leave us confused, some make us agitated—one of those is an attempt to copy others without proper consideration of the scope. It is a factor worthy of thought in any attempt to replicate a result. Some people ignore it and find themselves in an unpleasant situation.

Ideally, the result you desire may be dependent on so many factors. If they change, the end will change as well. It would be easy to duplicate any outcome if all of them remain the same—it is not always the case—if it ever was. They differ from people to people, from circumstance to circumstance, from group to group, and from time to time.

The Scope

It is possible to get the best result by carefully examining the sphere, extent, area, region, varieties, reach, size or range to which something is or not applicable. It is a piece of vital information that is not so obvious but can affect the output. An attempt to apply knowledge when the difference in scope is significant may lead to frustration. Many people that continued following others but ignored it were disappointed.

Some time ago, I found a digital image that looks good, but I wanted to make it bigger to fit into a larger frame using suitable software—the trial led to some discoveries. You may have found that there are usually some convenient arrows around the sides or edges, which you could move to expand the side or corners. It helps resize images to suit a different application. If you have tried it before, you may find that the image may get distorted if the expansion was not in line with the original ratio—the sides and edges must be moved in proportion to retain the quality. It implies that it is a crucial factor in producing that image in your desired size.

Moreover, I did resize it gradually—it seems fine as it preserved it in the right proportion—the picture still looks good and a little bigger. I tried to continue with the resizing to make it bigger than it was—I soon discovered that the image began to lose its quality—it was becoming blurred after the changes—differing gradually from the original image. The more I continued, the worse it became. I wonder if you have had such an experience.

I learnt something significant from the experience that can apply to what we do, imitate or replicate. We may desire to copy something that looks good or fascinating from one place, but an attempt to produce the same in a different place leads to a blurred imitation—the quality of the image gets lost in the process. It was good in its original application but distorted in the attempt to reproduce it.

The Scope

What other people are doing may look good, but it may be because it is in their size, you cannot make it bigger and retain the quality. You may not achieve the same thing in a bigger size, using the same features. There could be something that looks good on your friend, but if you try to do the same, it will look like a distortion because there is a difference that you have ignored. There is probably something different about your friend that made it fit. Conversely, it made it unfit for you.

Some things may work when the size is small or among the few, but the quality is lost when applied to a different scenario with big sizes. The idea may be good, but the difference in size may affect the result.

Consider three leaders, each having oversight of one, ten and a hundred people, respectively. They are all leaders, but their responsibilities grow as the number of people increases. The ratio is a crucial consideration, as what will make the leader of one a success may not be sufficient for a leader of a hundred. There are more considerations required to succeed when the numbers increases. The more the numbers, the more complicated it could be—the more details that appear—the more diverse it could become. You may not be able to apply the knowledge you get verbatim—you need to consider the difference and adapt it to meet the need. Sometimes, everything may not fit. You may adopt some, discard some or even discard everything to make your own to prevent distortion.

Have you had similar experiences? You probably saw something that worked for Mr A. You tried to do the same but never considered the situation in which it worked, but only found out that it did not work for you. It is often a good idea to understand the scope.

It explains why many solutions that work in a small environment will not necessarily produce the same result in a large one, except it is adapted to work in such places.

The Scope

Preparing dinner for five people may be challenging, but one person could produce a fantastic meal for them. However, there would be more considerations to achieve the same result in a larger gathering. There is a limitation to the strategy that worked with only one person—it may work well for five, but as the number of dinners multiplies to say a hundred or a thousand, the quality of service begins to diminish.

You may have found it to be true.

It may be a decision that worked for somebody you know at a particular time or season or an idea that perfectly fits one generation, or a style that became the highlight of an occasion. Yes, it was brilliant for the size and the time, but the quality and relevance may diminish when applied to something different or a new scenario or occasion.

A classroom of five students is different from a class of fifty. One teacher may have done well with five, but with more students or a different environment, the result may diminish if the approach is not adapted to fit the new size. An idea may yield great results because of the limited numbers, but the same may become distorted with large numbers if not adapted to fit.

Many years ago, a married couple had a baby girl as their first child. She grew up with little or no concerns. She listened and obeyed every instruction, sat quietly, and would not disturb anyone, most of the time. She would pass for a child that many refer to as a well-trained child. The mother soon concluded that she got the secret of raising well-trained children. Some others tried to copy her but could not get the same result with their children and were frustrated.

Some years later, they had another child, now a boy and thought it would be the same experience, but she discovered she was wrong. The boy was the exact opposite of the girl, and training him required understanding him as different from his sister.

The Scope

The mother did not understand the scope of her experience. She got to know the limitation of her approach when applied to a different child—a boy. The training of the first girl was easy for her, so she thought the method would work for others or all children, but she was wrong.

We may be frustrated when we copy other people—especially when there is a good outcome. It may be brilliant proof, but we may not appreciate that it is within a limited scope.

A particular medication might be a cure for a disease and probably used by some people that confirmed its efficacy. It does not mean that it is the best option for anyone with the same illness. There are so many factors that could make it unfit for other people. That is why doctors need to understand the constituents of the medication and its effects to know who can or should use it. The fact that it worked for one person does not mean it should be the prescription for everyone—it could end in disaster.

Many organisations invest so much to test the limits of their products. It is to ascertain who can use them and under what conditions. It would be dangerous to give it to everyone to use because one person has used it without problems. There are so many factors that can vary the outcome. They should be issues for consideration before being recommended for other people to use. So many people have had unpleasant experiences by doing things that other people do without paying attention to difference.

Research papers will usually define the scope—the limits of the problems to be investigated. In other words, if you want to follow or apply it, you need to do so within the stated boundaries to get the stipulated results. Every well-managed project also has the same, carefully documented—it defines the area of focus and the areas

The Scope

covered. It is very crucial for anyone that desires to learn from the work or outcome.

In every nation, there are laws, but they differ from one to another, which implies that what you do in one could be acceptable but wrong and probably an offence in another. The same action may have different interpretations because of the difference in location.

Germany's autobahn is one of the few public roads in the world without an official highway speed limit. In other words, you can travel as fast as you can, yet you do not break any law. However, if you cross the border to Switzerland, it is a different story—it is a criminal offence to go above the speed limit, and it comes with hefty fines.

A driver probably got one of those when he got caught in the act. It is a bill that could amount to over a million dollars—for driving above the limit in the country.[1] It explains the impact and cost of doing what other people do without considering the scope. In the former, the action was within the law but not in the latter.

You may have friends that waste money or live carelessly. The may never lack money probably because they have influential parents, but the same may not be your situation. If you do not understand your limits and live wisely, you may follow others in error and discover that you have robbed yourself of a great future.

Some students have friends that do not take their studies seriously—they disturb and distract. They may have lucrative jobs waiting for them, so their actions do not affect their job prospects or income later in life. They are in school for a different purpose, but some copy without understanding and waste their future by disregarding the opportunity to learn.

It is not everything that you are capable of doing that is good for you. You should not copy everything that people do. It may be suitable for someone else and probably lawful, but it may only be so because of where they are at the moment. The same action may put you in trouble or destroy you because of where you are, who you are or where you are going.

We are all different and unique. It is a truth that we should never forget. It will always help and guide us in the things we should do.

CHAPTER 20

The Use

Everything in life has its rightful place. The same is true of what we know. It is good to know, but how it benefits us depends on how we use or apply it.

I was in a Statistics class many years ago, and my teacher taught on a topic called Frequency in this specific class. It was interesting, but what caught my attention was different. I learnt a crucial lesson. He mentioned some use cases and acknowledged that there are many more ways that we may decide to use the knowledge. He said that some people use it to do evil while others use it for good.

Criminals may use it to monitor their victims, while Police may use it to monitor the criminals. You can use it to plan for

The Use

something that will add value to you or others. The same, interestingly, can be used to cause harm. It depends on how it is applied. It is amazing.

I learnt something new. It is not the source of the information that guarantees right or wrong. It is not where you get the information that determines whether you will become a better person. It is how you use the information that determines whether it adds to you or subtracts from you. One person uses it for criminal activity, while another uses it for something productive. It is not what you know but what you do with what you know that matters.

Consider an individual that stole building materials from a building site at night. He was successful because he has some skills—he would probably do well as a builder, plumber or carpenter during the day. He used the skills he had to steal instead.

A thief that could remove a pumping machine from a well at night would be more successful during the day. He knows how but decides to use it to cause loss or inconvenience for someone else.

Anyone that can successfully smuggle goods must be good in packaging. Anybody that could convince a stranger to willingly give their money in expectation of some goods or services that are not real must have some persuasive skills. What did they use it to achieve? They chose to use it for deceit.

Those that print fake money have some skills but used them to make counterfeit currencies. They would probably do well in a legitimate printing business.

A man that can beat his wife to a stupor may use the same resources to help in the army, but he chose not to do so. He used it to harm the one he claims to love.

The fraudsters that defraud people or deceive use their knowledge to cause harm. It could make the life of someone better if they chose to use it beneficially. The people that make software to steal personal

The Use

information or harm computers have some expertise, but they preferred to use it to cause harm rather than good.

Some individuals gain access to cars, either by creating an imitation key or intercepting the signal. They must have a good understanding of the technology involved, but they chose to use it for a purpose that hurts other people.

The knowledge can be beneficial in building people but can also be used to destroy. The skills that can help can also cause harm to people. The activity that brings profit can also cause losses. It is not just what you know that matters; what you do with it matters too.

Many have lost their life savings to some people that pretend to be friends or helpers. They show that they care and willing to help for a while to deceive and rob their victims. They know the effect of care, willingness and availability to help, but they use it to make their victims cry at the end.

What are you doing with your knowledge, skill and abilities? Are you causing harm or providing genuine benefit? What are you copying from others, and what are you doing with it? You can choose to make a difference and make the world a better place.

It is good to learn from others but do so with understanding. It is not only what you know that matters but also what you do.

It is not what you know but what you do with what you know that matters.

CHAPTER 21
The Need

One of the needs of humankind is knowledge. Everyone needs it, but many people do not realise that it is what they need. Some may assume they know enough, but their life may reveal some gaps that prove otherwise. Many people desire to know more, but some do not bother. Some others find it challenging to connect to some of the sources that could help them meet their need.

It is often true that some may never know enough to make them live a fulfilling life, and some others are frustrated while they are still alive because they do not know the right thing to do. They only know the wrong, what they feel or assume is right—and that is all they act upon in life. Every life is a function of how this need gets fulfilled.

The Need

There are innumerable opportunities to learn from other people in our world. You can significantly add value to your life by recognising and appreciating the enormous pool of human resources and gifts there are around us. The wealth of resources we have in people that have lived, combined with rich knowledge of those living, is enough, if well harnessed, to maximise your potential and fulfil your purpose.

It is vital to be sincere and truthful to oneself. It is crucial to recognise reality. No one knows everything, the wise keeps learning, and that makes them better still. Some will never maximise their potential if they continue to ignore others. Some others will not go further till they come out of the different barriers they have created for themselves. Prejudice has robbed many of a great future.

The answer you need may not all come from the same source. If you need help with your car—you approach the mechanic. If you need help with your teeth—approach the dentist. If you need help with your hair—you locate the salon. Someone somewhere has what you need. You need to appreciate that fact and seek the assistance that is available through them. You are not the first to live, and you will not be the last. Appreciate everyone for who they are and be willing to serve and be served.

A doctor can prescribe a medication to help a sick person get well. It is vital to know that he has invested over fourteen years of his life, learning the specialist skill from several people that have gone before him. He has also become a resource that can pass the same to other people interested in the same field of human endeavour. Many people do not know anything about the diseases that make them ill yet refuse to listen to a doctor that knows. They often suffer and sometimes cut their life short.

Some people have lived a frustrating life for fifty years but discovered something that changed their life by learning from those that have gone ahead. Their life changed when they knew something different, but it is better to find it out early in life to maximise time.

Several people have lived and attempted numerous things, some of which you plan to do or probably know nothing about yet. They have results to show for actions they took, which can educate you and help you make informed decisions. You can enhance your life by avoiding their mistakes and doing the right things.

There are some things you will never know in life until you are humble. You may need to learn from those you may think are below you. There are some things you may never understand until you can realise the way other people view things. Many things will never make sense to you until you venture into the worlds of others. It may not be clear to you why some people do what they do until you can stand in their shoes.

A few things may remain a mystery until you decide to be tough and dedicated. You may not know why some things happen until you can pay the price. You may never experience some until you can sacrifice. You may not know any better until you look beyond your locality, self, people, preferences, barriers, profession, or nationality. Many have been so limited and have short-changed themselves without knowing.

If you learn from the poor or rich, and it makes you a better person. You have gained, and no one can deny your result. The poverty or riches of the person may not affect the quality of the knowledge, but what you have gained will improve the quality of your life. It will not matter if it was from a known or unknown person as long as you can apply it aright. The knowledge is not faithful to whosoever had it first; it produces for anyone that uses it correctly and shows the evidence in an enhanced life. Do not despise the great help that is available to you.

Be wise as you learn from other people.

References

Preface

[1] D. McKeown, A. Luescher, and M. Machum, "Coprophagia: Food for Thought," *The Canadian Veterinary Journal*, vol. 29, no. 10, pp. 849–850, Oct. 1988, Accessed: Mar. 29, 2021. [Online]. Available: https://www.ncbi.nlm.nih.gov/pmc/articles/PMC1680886/.

Chapter 1: The Choice

[1] BBC, "The Schoolgirl Who Helped to Win a War," *www.bbc.co.uk*, Jul. 11, 2020. https://www.bbc.co.uk/iplayer/episode/m000kzx7/the-schoolgirl-who-helped-to-win-a-

war (accessed Jul. 13, 2020).

Chapter 10: The Purpose

[1] NIDA, "What Is cocaine?," *Drugabuse.gov*, May 01, 2016. https://www.drugabuse.gov/publications/research-reports/cocaine/what-cocaine (accessed Sep. 14, 2020).

[2] D. Sales, R. Tingle, and V. Chaudhary, "Married teacher, 35, Is Guilty of Having Sex with Her pupil, 15," *Mail Online*, Jan. 28, 2021. https://www.dailymail.co.uk/news/article-9189047/Married-teacher-35-guilty-having-sex-15-year-old-pupil-adding-Snapchat.html (accessed Apr. 02, 2021).

Chapter 11: The Inverse

[1] A. Hunt and B. Wheeler, "10 Ways the PM Blew Her Majority," *BBC News*, Jun. 14, 2017.

[2] BBC, "Election Results 2019: Tories Take Labour Seats as They Head for Majority," *BBC News*, Dec. 13, 2019.

Chapter 19: The Scope

[1] T. Stephens, "Driver Faces $1,000,000 Speeding Fine," *SWI swissinfo.ch*, Aug. 13, 2010. https://www.swissinfo.ch/eng/driver-faces--1-000-000-speeding-fine/23091098 (accessed Apr. 30, 2021).

Thank you

Thank you for investing in this book. I hope you enjoyed reading it as much as it has been a pleasure for me to write it, and I trust that it has helped you.

It would be helpful to me and many others if you could share your experience by way of a review or a comment.

Please write to:

iph@TheServantandKing.com

We would be glad to hear from you.

Looking for more?

Please visit:

www.TheServantandKing.com

Automated: The concept of continuous results with diminishing involvement.

IF YOU KEEP DOING THE SAME THING
OVER AND OVER AGAIN AND EXPECTING
THE SAME RESULT: THINK AUTOMATION.

Let this book inspire you to productivity!

Available on Amazon or your local bookstore.

Recover: Finding Help in times of need.

IT SEEMS THAT WITHOUT GOD, MAN CANNOT
AND WITHOUT MAN, GOD WILL NOT.
— JOHN WESLEY

Recover, packed with real stories and recommended actions, will help you in your journey to navigate your present or future challenges to fulfil your potential.

Available on Amazon or your local bookstore.

Essential: Finding Relevance in the Midst of Crisis

WHEN ONE DOOR CLOSES
ANOTHER DOOR OPENS; BUT WE SO OFTEN LOOK
SO LONG AND SO REGRETFULLY UPON THE CLOSED
DOOR, THAT WE DO NOT SEE THE ONES WHICH OPEN FOR US.
— ALEXANDER GRAHAM BELL

In Essential, you will find some clear and actionable advice that will help to restore hope and encourage you to step out and make the most of any situation. You are essential because you can make yourself relevant even when things change.

Available on Amazon or your local bookstore.

www.ingramcontent.com/pod-product-compliance
Lightning Source LLC
Chambersburg PA
CBHW060519100426
42743CB00009B/1383